WITHOUT FAIL, RECOVER ALL

SPIRITUAL PRINCIPLES TO ACTIVATE RECOVERY IN BUSINESS

---

by Allan Rockhill

WITHOUT FAIL, RECOVER ALL
SPIRITUAL PRINCIPLES TO ACTIVATE RECOVERY IN BUSINESS

Published by Total Fusion Press
6475 Cherry Run Rd. Strasburg, OH 44680
www.totalfusionpress.com

Printed in the United States of America
25 24 23 22 21 20 19 18 17 16   1 2 3 4 5

ISBN – 10:1-943496-04-8
ISBN-13:978-1-943496-04-4

Cover Design by Terry Ladrach
Edited by Andrea Long

Published in Association with Total Fusion Ministries, Strasburg, OH.
www.totalfusionministries.org

Dedication

This book is dedicated to all of God's market-related kings-in-business, who fall on tough times in uncertain economic seasons, and who may need to find assistance on the road to recovery. Whilst the practice of sound business ethics on the ground remains paramount and a foregone conclusion in the writing of this book, these **spiritual recovery principles** will assist in broadening your understanding and reveal more of God's financial arsenal that is at your disposal. Knowing how to apply these spiritual concepts with understanding, in addition to your natural skill when operating business, will hasten recovery. We must have both these arms in good working order.

Diligence to God's financial principles and economic strategies and a **disciplined** work ethic will produce **recovery** in unprecedented proportions.

God could not leave Hagar to die in the desert, nor Elijah under the juniper tree. He could not leave the four lepers in a siege with no hope. Likewise, His call on your financial kingship remains intact. He has a recovery plan for those who need it.

God has appointed you as a king-in-business in the marketplace and delights in seeing you prosper into your calling and destiny. The thoughts contained in this publication are particularly for YOU. May God assist you in recovering the sharpness of your axe-head and once again help you discover the paths that will lead you to a full recovery in your business.

Table of Contents

Table of Contents

Preface

David grew from the position of a shepherd boy to being God's chosen king over Israel. He grew from being the youngest in his family (therefore overlooked by his father when it came to significance) to rule over people, nations, and situations that presented themselves. He became a king. His stature was immense and his word as a king was final.

He was no stranger to war and personal battles, and whilst he enjoyed some incredible triumphs, he also knew what it was to lose and suffer defeat. He understood the anguish and pain that life brought on. What made him exceptional as a leader was not only the number of victories he amassed, but also the way he **recovered** when he was broken or suffered defeat.

Recovery is a process which God wants His marketplace kings-in-business to discover and experience more and more. At one the lowest times in David's life, when he and his mighty men suffered great stress and anxiety at the probable loss of their wives and children, emotions were so highly charged that these faithful men even thought of stoning him. David immediately went to seek the Lord for advice and what God gave him changed the whole outcome:

> **So David inquired of the Lord, saying, "Shall I pursue this troop? Shall I overtake them?" And He answered him, "Pursue, for you shall surely overtake them and without fail recover all."**
> **(1 Samuel 30:8)**

The road to recovery is a battle God's financial kings must learn to embrace and know how to conquer. They need to have strategy to be able to recover all that has been taken or stolen from them. A financial king's destiny is to plunder the wealth of the world and to allow generous portions of it to pass into the church and kingdom of God, enabling the church to finance the reaching of the lost and God's purposes in the relevant communities. Financial difficulties and pressures do form part of the regular life of those in business and many suffer dangerous loss and even capitulate when under sustained attack.

Learning to **recover** and get back what has been stolen or steered away from your kingship is an essential key a king-in-business must possess. He must know how to turn things around in God and not allow the desires of our archenemy to settle in his businesses. God made us the **head** and not the **tail**. The spirit of Caleb, **"We are well able to possess what God has given us,"** must prevail. **(Num 13:30)**

Introduction

This book is written to a group of people in the body of Christ that are dear to my heart. They have such a significant role to play in assisting the furthering of the kingdom of God and the impact a local church has on its community. These people are **God's Financial Kings**, chosen to plunder markets and tithe portions of their profits into the purpose of the church on the earth. If you are reading this book, I assume that you understand this calling and if in the case of recovery being required, then this book is written for you.

Financial kings are often misused in the body and many have become the targets of unrighteous leaders, suffering financial abuse and resulting in large numbers leaving the church disillusioned. Times and seasons also get hard for these marketplace kings and they often wilt under this mounting pressure. Some have seriously lost heart and their sense of purpose and yet they still remain in the forefront of God's plan to finance the purposes of the kingdom. The gifts and callings of God are irrevocable **(Rom 11:29)**. The words that are penned here are to give these people hope and re-ignite the understanding of their value and significant purpose from God. These functioning gifts in the body of Christ are crucial to the advancement of the church and the kingdom of God.

Whilst good and prosperous seasons are part of the business king's profile, hard and lean times are sadly part of that same equation. The unpredictable changes that occur in the marketplace affect business kings and play havoc on their performance on the ground. Uncertain economies, crashed markets, and recessions, for example, really affect buying and selling, which in turn places huge pressure on budgets and targets. If this pressure remains for awhile, it can lead to cut backs in company operations, reduction in staff, shorter working weeks, and no credit at banks. Cash flow will be affected and those who do not have sufficient funds will be in serious trouble—forced to look for ways to downsize in every department.

The world economic recession of 2008 and onwards is a case in point. Business in all forms—from large companies to the entrepreneur on the ground—felt the toughness of that season. Many went bankrupt and many others are still feeling the effect of that time today. Economists tell us that worse is still to come.

What God's business kings should keep close to their hearts is that they serve a God who is master over the impossible. He is never caught without options or solutions that lead to recovery. Adam and Eve were right up there in His recovery statistics. Eve, who was called that because she **"...was the mother of all living..." (Gen 3:20)** lost her son Abel in a fit of jealousy. Cain, his brother, killed him one day out in the fields and this act devastated the meaning of her existence. But God was on hand to encourage her, and when another son was born, he was called **Seth**, meaning, *"one appointed to take the place of"* **(Gen 4:25)**. God provided a solution to keep the original plan in place. He always has a replacement option to keep things moving as they were intended.

God's financial kings should learn from this example. They are in place at the appointment of God. He knows the uncertainty in the world's economic markets and how difficult and uncertain they can be from time to time. Knowing God and having a relationship with Him that is real and not just mechanical, is part of the key recovery tactics that any business king should be familiar with. Unless you know what God is saying and how He is leading you, finding the solutions to recover fully become extremely difficult.

David also understood what it was to be completely devastated by circumstances. He knew what it was to feel the pain of losing it all. Even though he had done all he could to secure the safety of his family and those he was responsible for, they were still captured in an enemy raid. The chances of them being found alive were very slim. He and his mighty men wept bitterly in their anguish, **"...until they had no more power to weep."** (1 Sam 30:4) Even though these circumstances were hard to contend with, David had a relationship with God where he **"...strengthened himself in the Lord his God"** (1 Sam 30:6) He needed to have an answer from God or a plan of action that would lead to their recovery. He heard God say, **"'Pursue, for you shall surely overtake them and without fail recover all.'"** (1 Sam 30:8)

This reply was so good on a number of levels. David was reassured that:

1) Their families were alive
2) They were not unreachable
3) They would not fail to recover ALL they had lost

What a soothing word to receive from God when he was so broken and unsure of the way forward. What a word to bring to his mighty men in their state of despair, as well. It was this promise that changed the whole outcome. This instruction from God was their solution, which would lead to them **recovering all.** You as the CEO or director of your company need to be able to step out of the ashes when things are really tough economically, and be able to tell your employees that God has promised recovery and this is His plan.

May the principles penned in this writing inspire and activate your personal recovery and lead you to new levels of breakthrough in your calling as business kings for God. May God bless your endeavours and make your way prosperous to your destiny of financial wealth and stability. May your generosity assist the purpose of the church in being effective in advancing the Kingdom of God on the earth. A significant amount of its advance rests on the success of your function in the body of Christ. You are not just a chequebook. You are a planned purpose of God, set in the ranks of the local church, able to assist in its impact for God.

To learn more about your role as a business king in the marketplace, please see the book *Financial Kingship: Principles to Unleash Kings in the Marketplace*, also by Allan Rockhill (published by Total Fusion Press, 2013).

Chapter One

ALERT TO WHAT GOD WILL SEND

Then Elisha went to Damascus, and Ben-Hadad king of Syria was sick; and it was told him, saying, "The man of God has come here." And the king said to Hazael, "Take a present in your hand, and go to meet the man of God, and inquire of the Lord by him, saying, 'Shall I recover from this disease?'"**

(2 Kings 8:7-8)

OPPORTUNITY ALWAYS PRESENTS ITSELF

An amazing fact about God is that He always has a way forward for us to discover. Once you know the plan or hear the Word on how to do things, you must activate the plan. Recovery depends largely on being able to recognize what opportunities have presented themselves in your situation. In this portion of scripture, Ben-Hadad was the king of Syria. He was the leading figure in the nation. He had become physically ill and it appeared to be quite serious, as he wanted to know if he would recover from his condition. **(v8)**

It was also relayed to Ben-Hadad that, **"The man of God has come here." (v7)** One of the spiritual keys to seeing recovery in business is based on the emphasis and value that is placed on the **man of God** who is sent into your life. These gift ministries carry an anointing from God that are able to supernaturally change the course of things in your business. They also release the value and power of the **rhema word** that not even the gates of Hades can withstand. The rhema words they release are the **'now'** words that bring life and are the words that Jesus told us we should live on. **(Matt 4:4)** They may on the other hand just offer sound biblical sense for you to activate and your responses of faith will determine the measure of your breakthrough and recovery.

Think back in the Word of God—how many people, who knew that when a prophet of God was in the vicinity, or knew that Jesus himself was going to pass by, responded in faith and expectation to the opportunity that had arisen? Many people crowded Jesus, wanting Him to just touch them so they could be healed, and no one was ever disappointed. Let's be reminded of:

1) **Naaman**, the Syrian general who had leprosy and who listened and responded to the voice of a young slave girl in his house. **(2 Kings 5)**
2) **Zaccheus**, a short man, who climbed up a tree because he wanted to see Jesus. He found out the route Jesus was taking out of Jericho and waited in a tree in anticipation of seeing Him whom everyone was speaking about. **(Luke 19)**
3) The **Syro-Phonecian** woman who was willing to accept a few crumbs from the table as sufficient for her great need. **(Mark 7) (Matt. 15)**
4) Blind **Bartimaeus** who was prepared to make a fool of himself and against advice, shouted above the voices in the crowd. **(Mark 10)**

All these people activated a faith response to the sent opportunity they were presented and went away completely satisfied. A prophet in his hometown was all the opportunity Ben-Hadad needed. God had sent a gift ministry in close proximity to the needy king.

It would be wise for business kings to realize the value of the man of God in their lives. He is a gift to them. Ongoing business success, recovery in business, or failed business has a direct bearing on the spiritual influence you accept into your life. **Psalm 92:13-14** tells us, **"Those who are planted in the house of the Lord shall flourish in the courts of our God. They shall still bear fruit in old age; They shall be fresh and flourishing."** Financial Kings are a part of those who can be planted. They are a definite plan of God for a church. God wants them planted in a house of God, under a gift ministry, where there is accountability and relationship and where the gift anointing in the set man can operate continuously in their favour. Financial success in the marketplace is also proportional to the business king's attitude and response to what God has placed in spiritual authority over him. The moment Ben-Hadad heard that God had sent Elisha into his area, he responded to the opportunity presented.

Having been a pastor for many years and now travelling extensively around the world to help the body of Christ where I can, it saddens me to see how many struggling pastors and their business kings allow this type of opportunity (financial mentors, prophetic ministries, etc.) to pass them by. God sends a gift ministry to their location and they pass it off, easily surrendering the opportunity that a revelatory word, a prophetic word or even a rhema (now) word, could have on their situation. In my understanding, this is just not smart. If God has an answer or an opportunity for you, how can there be an indifferent response to it? Let's remind ourselves that **Naaman** would have remained a leper unless he responded by activating his faith to the cry of the little servant girl's voice. **Bartimaeus** would have stayed a blind man had he listened to the voices of the crowd around him. Instead he realized that this was his **sent opportunity**—his moment to change things from the way they were. No crowd with their view or opinion on his condition would stop his opportunity. This was his moment and he was going to seize it with both hands.

In **Genesis 41**, Pharaoh had experienced some troublesome dreams; and yet he knew they were related in some way to Egypt's destiny. He needed these dreams accurately interpreted. He discovered that all of his learned people and those who dabbled in the occult world did not have the correct interpretation. The only possible candidate was a prisoner called Joseph. Now here was a Hebrew, an unkempt prisoner in the king's prison (which normally meant they were a serious threat to the nation), right on Pharaoh's doorstep. Those who served him at close hand had told him that this man, Joseph, had the gift of interpreting dreams. HERE WAS HIS SENT OPPORTUNITY, but it was also one of his greatest challenges. Does a king over a nation take advice from a Hebrew slave locked away in his prison? What would the neighbouring kings around him think? What would it do to his reputation as a respected leader in their part of the world? Does a renowned king take council from those in his prison and not from his esteemed advisory council that he appointed?

Pharaoh had a choice. God had presented an opportunity to him. It was not what he would normally have considered, but it was a resource he was glad he entertained. Joseph interpreted the dreams and provided a strategic plan for Pharaoh to not only save Egypt from the impending famine, but to help the known world at the same time. This strategy was also an economic blessing to Egypt. Promoting Joseph to second in charge kept them alive and contributed to Egypt becoming a super power at that time.

Do you want to recover financially? Do you want to be healed from sickness? Do you want breakthrough in your circumstances? Has God sent to your vicinity a gift ministry or a man from God who has His Spirit in him? **(Gen 41:38)** Are you planted under an anointing of a set man? Responding in faith and with expectation to the leading of God through them, are keys that lead to recovery where it is needed. Make sure you elevate the effect these gift people can have on you. Take their anointing seriously. It has the power to cause recovery in your business situation.

> **"...Believe in the Lord your God, and you shall be established; believe His prophets, and you shall prosper"**
> **(2 Chron 20:20)**

IT WILL COST

Another step to activate ongoing success or recovery in business is always to understand exactly how the key of generosity works. The one aspect that separates financial kings from other groups of people is not only their ability to rule and provide solutions to seemingly impossible situations, but also their desire to be generous even when under financial pressure.

> **"The generous soul will be made rich, And he who waters will also be watered himself."**
> **(Proverbs 11: 25)**

17

No business king will ever reach the financial blessing God has designed, unless he is a generous giver, connected to a man of God in his life, and becomes a sent gift himself. God blesses you to send help to others in need. It goes without saying that financial kings need to be generous, and when they are the promise of God to them is that they also will be refreshed when necessary. The measure they use to refresh others is the same measure that will come back. God wants His business kings wealthy. In fact a business king's purpose is to be a conduit of financial blessing into the kingdom. He is anointed to amass this wealth and God takes pleasure in his prosperity. In the book of **Deuteronomy**, God lays down a whole discourse of the blessing He wanted Israel to enjoy when they got to the Promised Land. God endorsed this when He said:

> **"And you shall remember the Lord your God, for it is He who gives you power to get wealth, that He may establish His covenant which He swore to your fathers, as it is this day."**
> **(Deuteronomy 8:18)**

God always has purpose attached to the need of His business kings growing and prospering. However, successful business kings also understand that the honour (financial value) they attach to receiving from a sent man of God, is in proportion to the measure of the breakthrough they will experience.

David was a significant king in Israel and could have had anything he wanted. When he came to Araunah, who was the owner of the threshing floor where David needed to build an altar to the Lord, Araunah was more than willing to give the floor space to his king. It would have been an honour to do so. But David replied:

"...No, but I will surely buy it from you for a price; nor will I offer burnt offerings to the Lord my God with that which costs me nothing"

(2 Samuel 24:24)

David understood the principle that in order to receive, there needed to be a sacrifice sown from his part. He made sure that it was a personal cost to him and not money from the treasury. All through the Word of God we see this principle working:

1) **Genesis 18:3-5** Abraham served the three men that came from God.
2) **Judges 6:18** Gideon brought his personal offering.
3) **Judges 13:19** Manoah set his offering up for the visitation he had.
4) **1 Samuel 9:7** Saul wouldn't go to the Prophet without taking an offering.
5) 5) **2 Kings 5:15** Naaman took a gift to Elisha.
6) **2 Chronicles 9:24** Kings who came to Solomon brought gifts.
7) **Philippians 4:15-19** The Philippians supported Paul on God's business.

These are some of the clearest principles of financial breakthrough and recovery in business written in the Word of God. Don't go to receive from a sent gift ministry from God without taking an offering that would cost you personally. Place honour on what God sends you by taking a gift that has the measure of what you desire to receive.

Ben-Hadad needed to know if he would recover from the illness he had contracted. A man of God, Elisha, with a proven prophetic gift, and now 'a sent opportunity,' was in his town. He needed to approach him to find out if he would be healed.

19

There never was a doubt in Ben-Hadad's mind about
sending a gift. This was a sent ministry right into his area.
He would not go empty-handed. So he instructed Hazael:

> **"Take a present in your hand, and go to
> meet the man of God, and inquire of
> the Lord by him, saying, 'Shall I recover
> from this disease?'"**
>
> **(2 Kings 8:8)**

Notice the response from Hazael. He understood the
principle and took a gift with him. It was not a sub-standard
gift. Everything about it was generous. It seemed that the
people of that day understood the value of a man of God or
a ministry gift and were eager to lavish honour on them,
showing the acceptance of the principle that the measure
you use will be measured back to you.

> **So Hazael went to meet him and took a
> present with him, of every good thing of
> Damascus, forty camel-loads; and he
> came and stood before him, and said,
> "Your son Ben-Hadad king of Syria has
> sent me to you, saying, 'Shall I recover
> from this disease?'"**
>
> **(2 Kings 8:9)**

This is also what Naaman, the Syrian general did when he
went in search of Elisha. He had contracted leprosy and a
little maid (a captive of Israel) in his home told him of the
prophet of God in Israel who would heal him. He remembered this principle as he packed to go in search of him:

...So he departed and took with him ten talents of silver, six thousand shekels of gold, and ten changes of clothing.

(2 Kings 5:5)

This principle of taking a gift to the man of God sent to your area was an automatic response in those times. It had to cost you personally. You never went to a gift man of God empty-handed. This is a principle that must be restored to active financial kingship. It has such mammoth significance in breakthrough and maintaining a standard of ongoing success. After Naaman was healed, he returned to Elisha to thank him and to leave his gift with him. **(2 Kings 5:15)** He appreciated the role Elisha played before God to see his healing enacted.

I wonder how many of God's kings show their appreciation for successes that have had a lot to do with their men of God? Your set men (priests) pray for you and speak blessing over you to succeed. They arrange prophets to visit and speak a 'now' word over you and do what they can to see their kings-in-business prosper in the marketplace. Sadly not all kings respond correctly with the fruit of their blessings and not all bring the proper tithe into the storehouses as a result of their fruitful plunder. Ongoing business success, and even recovery, requires a re-look at this amazing principle and automatic response in people of that time.

God surrounds you with the gifting you will require to operate successfully in the marketplace, and showing thanks for what God has done for you should be a distinct consideration. Jesus once healed ten lepers and only one of them returned to say thank you. He asked only one question, **"Where are the other nine?" (Luke 17:11-19)**.

BE AWARE OF THE SMOTHERING TACTICS OF THE ENEMY

Hazael returned with the message, **"You shall certainly recover" (2 Kings 8:10)** and this Word would have relaxed Ben-Hadad and caused him to lower his guard for a brief moment. It was what he needed to hear, considering what he was going through. However, this promise of restoration also became an opportunity for an attack. Ben-Hadad was still physically weak even after he had the promise of a full recovery, and that is when the enemy struck. This is where God's financial kings need to remain consciously alert.

> **But it happened on the next day that he took a thick cloth and dipped it in water, and spread it over his face so that he died; and Hazael reigned in his place.**
> **(2 Kings 8:15)**

When your business has been seriously hindered and your existence is hanging on by a thread, it is wonderful to receive a word of recovery, just like Ben-Hadad. Though your spirit rejuvenates, you must remember that your flesh is still weak, which is when your enemy is likely to strike. There is no better way to demoralize a business king than to keep smothering him with failure, especially in the face of a promised recovery. This is what Hazael did to Ben-Hadad. It wasn't the original illness that killed him, but the selfish act of one who saw an opportunity to seize something desired, from one who had now relaxed his guard because of the exciting news of his promised recovery.

Financial kings still need to remain alert when God's promises of recovery are heard, keeping their faith, expectations, and declarations as a focus.

"...Believe in the Lord your God, and you shall be established; believe His prophets, and you shall prosper."

(2 Chronicles 20:20)

The devil will always try to smother what God has said about your recovery, until you lose your hope and confidence in that it will actually take place. His tactic is to make you feel you are still drowning and going under, regardless. He sees to it that a wet cloth to induce the sense of smothering covers your eyes, ears, mouth, and nose. His purpose is to interfere with your **vision** and **perception** so that you won't **speak** or **activate** in faith what you have been told.

It's important for financial kings to consider that there is normally a time period for your businesses to turn around. There is still some work to be done to lift you out of where you have been, when the word of recovery arrives. It would be wise to remember that these moments are possible opportunities for the enemy to loose his smothering tactics. When Jesus was tempted in the desert for forty days and nights **(Luke 4:1-13)**, it was at His weakest moment that the devil sent his temptations. Jesus, being conscious of God and actively declaring His Word, overcame this tough encounter. Though you may feel weak from struggling for a long time, keep your spirit man alert and focused on God. Keep alive:

1) Your vision
2) Your spoken dreams and expectations
3) Your rhema words from God
4) Your spiritual sensitivity to know what to do next
5) Your promise of recovery

You need to remember that you are on God's economic agenda despite what happens in the marketplace. God is not subject to how the world conducts its business affairs. He has His own strategy that is immune to what the world does. It's up to the financial kings to discover how to access that agenda. God is always your resource and still able to cause you to prosper, even if He tells you to sow in the midst of a financial drought **(Gen 26:1-3; 12-16)**. Just be wise and aware of the devil's tactics when you are still weak but have had the promise of business recovery. Be alert to the 'sent opportunities' that come to your doorstep and take an offering with you to show your respect and thanks for God's kindness to you.

Recovery is not for other people. It's for you. Ask the Holy Spirit to help you be sensitive to know when the opportunity that comes, is a sent one from God.

Chapter Two

MAKE ROOM FOR GOD'S MAN IN YOUR LIFE

Now it happened one day that Elisha went to Shunem, where there was a notable woman, and she persuaded him to eat some food. So it was, as often as he passed by, he would turn in there to eat some food. And she said to her husband, "Look now, I know that this is a holy man of God, who passes by us regularly. Please, let us make a small upper room on the wall; and let us put a bed for him there, and a table and a chair and a lampstand; so it will be, whenever he comes to us, he can turn in there."

(2 Kings 4:8-10)

EMBRACE WHAT YOU SEE GOD DOING

We read of the Shunammite woman in our story, that she was **notable** and **persuasive. (v8)** She was a woman of standing in her community and together with her husband, carried respect and authority. The word **notable** means *great, exceeding, and valuable.* It seems that once she saw a need or an opportunity she would fix her eyes on to it and work with it until a solution was found to utilize it.

She saw quickly enough that Elisha, a holy man of God, visited Shunem regularly and perceived the importance of this prophet to their city. She embraced what she saw God doing and immediately set about wanting to provide and care for him. She managed firstly to persuade him, whilst on his rounds for God, to accept their hospitality of a decent meal. She recognized the value of a prophet of God coming to their city and what he carried from God would be welcomed to stay awhile. This was a man who was used by God to speak His oracles and declare the Word of the Lord with amazing confirmations. It was a quality that was not only a current **now** word, but had **generational** blessing attached to it as well. God was delivering this opportunity to their city and she made **room** for him to stay at their home. This was a God moment not to be missed.

Recognizing the anointing God has brought into the proximity should inspire you, as it did the Shunammite. She positioned herself to accept this gift ministry. Here is a man that hears from heaven's throne room and speaks what God says. His words do not fall empty to the ground. Here is an opportunity to **embrace** a current now word, which God is allowing to come past your doorstep or within your grasp. The Shunammite saw all this and set about planning to have more of this anointing not only in her city, but also in her home.

MAKE ROOM FOR GOD'S OPPORTUNITY

Once you recognize what God is doing for you, the most profitable move is to ensure that you, your family, or your business become exposed to as much of this anointing as possible. Welcome these opportunities and **make room** for them by embracing them with both hands. The Shunammite woman, in agreement with her husband, **prepared a room** in their home where Elisha could stay and rest awhile before continuing on his journey for God. **(v10)** She was determined to be as close to this unique opportunity as possible. She wanted to benefit from any firsthand revelation, any morsel of life, or any inspiration that would give direction, confirmation, or reference to point them towards their destiny and purpose in God. Little did she realize how this action of **making room for her man of God** would benefit them later on.

Elisha was used by God in incredible ways wherever he went. He carried such a powerful anointing and sensitivity to the Spirit of God, that to be around him created the expectation that at any moment you could receive something out of heaven that would change your life completely. He was a true prophet of the Lord that spoke the Word of God in every situation. What he said was from God, would always be fulfilled, even if he was no longer alive. We find in **2 Kings 13:20-21** that a man was lowered into the tomb of Elisha by mistake, and when his body touched the bones of Elisha, **"...he revived and stood on his feet." (v21)** The power of the anointed word spoken does not lose its effectiveness through time spans. They have a time to be realized. The Prophet Isaiah spoke about a son that was to be given **(Isa 9:6)** approximately 800-1000 years before Jesus was born. Your prophetic word from God doesn't wane with time.

The prophetic works both now and beyond our time span. So **making room** for what God has sent to you is the best advice a person or king-in-business can respond to. It's not something that you nonchalantly do. Believing God's prophets is a release of personal prosperity for you **(2 Chron 20:20)**. It makes good sense to position yourself to hear from this gift ministry, and then embrace it. The Shunammite made room for Elisha because she was clear what that value would be to her and her family. In her case it led to a **generational blessing**. God is not a respecter of persons **(Acts 10:34)** and what He has already done for one, He can do for you as well.

Looking at where you are placed in your circumstances, where can you **make room for the man of God in your life?** This is the catalyst that will initiate change and recovery.

GOD IS NO MAN'S DEBTOR

When business kings pursue and make room for the ministry and prophetic revelation of their men of God, they place themselves in a very healthy position. God's anointing breaks the yoke **(Isa 10:27)** and His blessing spoken through these gifts, extends and creates new boundaries and opportunities to recover and continue in ongoing success. These 'gift ministries' have the ability to initiate turning points that will take your business to new heights.

The Shunammite family had now made room and been caring for Elisha and his servant for some time. They had consistently honoured what God had sent to them and this respect led to miraculous opportunities. In this particular case, the miraculous touched an area of recovery that had been put to bed as a **not going to happen** event. (I'll cover this in more detail in Chapter 3.)

> **And he said to him, "Say now to her, 'Look, you have been concerned for us with all this care. What can I do for you? Do you want me to speak on your behalf to the king or to the commander of the army?'" She answered, "I dwell among my own people."**

> **(2 Kings 4:13)**

Elisha came down from his room one day and quite unexpectedly addressed an area that was sensitive and personal to this family's ongoing success and generational life span. God is no man's debtor. Those who serve God and honour what He sends you will be repaid and rewarded by Him in a way that is way beyond what you could have expected. He is a good God and His goodness cannot be boxed in our mind-sets.

Elisha asks, **"What can I do for you?" (v13)**. He was basically saying: *You have taken care of me so well. You have respected the anointing in me and made room for it. Is there something I can do for you? Is there a problem that you can't fix? I can speak to the king or even the commander of the army for you.* Prophets carried the highest authority in the natural world the Shunammite woman could ever want. Imagine a prophet of Elisha's pedigree saying to you, "What can I do for you?" This is a man of God with a proven track record of one who hears from God, and here he is saying to you, "What can I do for you?"

To recover in business or to keep going in continual success mode, we must answer the question, "How much room have I made for my man of God and his anointing in my life?" God will come through for you according to the value you place on His anointing in this gift ministry.

Chapter Three

THE SHUNAMMITE'S GENERATIONAL BLESSING

So he said, "What then is to be done for her?" And Gehazi answered, "Actually, she has no son, and her husband is old."

(2 Kings 4:14)

Then Elisha spoke to the woman whose son he had restored to life, saying, "Arise and go, you and your household, and stay wherever you can; for the Lord has called for a famine, and furthermore, it will come upon the land for seven years."

(2 Kings 8:1)

POSITIONED FOR BLESSING

Right from our introduction to the Shunammite woman, we see a servant heart and a desire to have Elisha, the man of God in her life, as a regular visitor in her home. There was no hiding the fact that she honoured the prophet and consequently would receive the prophet's reward **(Matt 10:41)**. She obviously had insight into the value of this gift ministry and positioned herself accordingly:

    1)   She believed Elijah was a sent man from God.

2) As a sent man, he carried a unique but authentic gift that came out of throne room of heaven.

3) Caring for him was important to God, and therefore the right thing to do.

4) She had to make room for this anointing.

Little did she realize that this attitude positioned her for rewards that would span generations. Financial kings operate in the toughest arena known to man and should adopt a similar stance. They are up against all levels of cunning and debauchery that thrive in the marketplace, brought on by greed. When a king-in-business starts his day, it's almost like he is off to a war zone. **Normal people go to work, but kings go to war**. You contend with the highest forms of self-preservation, where schemes and deals are engineered to satisfy and suit what people want. Survival for those in the marketplace often comes at a price that you are forced to pay. It makes perfect sense that a business king should be positioned correctly if he is to withstand the pressures and goings-on of the marketplace.

A key ingredient to succeed in this environment is wrapped up in the **mantle** (or protective covering) of God's gift man in your situation. Making room for what God has supplied for you to grow and prosper is wise and gets you positioned correctly to receive the **downloads** (words from God) that will underline your success and keep you pointed in the right direction.

THE SHUNNAMMITE'S REWARDS THAT SPANNED GENERATIONS (2 KINGS 4:8-37)

1. "What can I do for you?" (v13)

God is no man's debtor. The principle of, **"Give and it shall be given unto you" (Luke 6:38)**, is a key to see the release of God in your circumstances. The four lepers first had to get up and move towards the Syrian camp **(2 Kings 7:3)** before God showed His hand. There must be movement in faith before God will act. That is why if you want to see a harvest in your finances, the word encourages sowing first. God always responds when He sees your faith in action. This Shunammite woman made room for God's man by caring for him and his servant with excellence and it led to the reward a little later of, **"What can I do for you?"** What a blessing to have a man of God of that caliber say this! It came as a response to how she had first moved in Elisha's situation.

Business kings who have experienced failure, hardship, or are on the brink of bankruptcy, and who want to see recovery and ongoing success now and in the future, would do well to take a leaf out of this lady's book. Honour and place value on the gift man that God has sent to shape and direct your financial destiny. Serving and making room for this gift is a wise position to adopt. It will have long-term results that reveal God's favour.

2. **"Do you want me to speak on your behalf to the king…?" (v13)**

Elisha moved in hierarchical circles as well. When you carry an anointing from God, all levels of society want to benefit—including kings of nations and the very ordinary. All levels of people need what you carry. The offer of the king's involvement was an extraordinary one. The king obviously knew Elisha personally for him to offer this opportunity to someone outside of those circles. He was the highest authority available and Elisha was prepared to ask for his assistance, in case it was needed.

The implication is that being close to a prophet of God, the man God has sent your way and the one you have made room for in your life and circumstances, means having access to levels of society that have the power to make things happen or not. The king of any nation in biblical times had just to say a word and it would be done. This is what Elisha was offering to her. He was saying, *The way you have made room and cared for me means I can do the same for you, should you require it.*

3. **"Do you want me to speak on your behalf… to the commander of the army?" (v13)**

Elisha also offered the help of the highest authority in the army. If she had some battles that needed overcoming and was struggling to achieve them, he was able to chat to the commanding General of the Army. He had at his command the latest weaponry and manpower resources she could ever wish for. With this kind of support backing her, her enemies would dissipate and think twice before standing in opposition to her.

By implication, I am sure many of God's business kings would love to have available to them the muscle to deal with twisted, cunning, and deceptive people that populate the marketplace. To have the measure on **"the wiles of the devil" (Eph 6:11)** is a most satisfying place to be. Thankfully these financial kings do not have to stoop to these levels to buy protection or force favour to get ahead in the market arena. God is all the resource you will ever need. He has all the muscle to protect His investment on the earth and has declared to us that, **"No weapon formed against you shall prosper…" (Isa 54:17)**

4. "...she has no son and her husband is old." (v14)

The Shunammite didn't require any help from the king or the commander of the army as her family stood together and provided whatever was needed. However, the question of reward and blessing was still outstanding, **"What then is to be done for her?"** (v14) Elisha was looking for a way to reward her kindness.

Without a son the generational influence ceases. Without a son there is no continued lineage. The purpose of that family would end with the death of the husband who was now old. God introduced Himself to us as a generational God. He is interested in a family line, growing through time and achieving all He has desired. That is why the concept of **fathers and sons** is so high on God's agenda. This is what Gehazi points out to Elisha. This family has no heir to fulfill the plans of God. To rectify this would have been the highest priority.

Entertaining the man of God in your life doesn't just help you relate to current circumstances. The moment you make that connection and serve the purpose why God brought this gift to you, you step into generational dynamics. You birth something that has the ability to perpetuate your future destiny as a family and business.

Whilst David was hiding in the Cave of Adullam, people who were in **d**ebt, **d**espair and **d**istress gathered to him and he became the **captain** over them. He trained them and took them from where they were with no hope of a future, to a mighty army that did amazing exploits for God. They connected with their gift man from God, even though it began in a cave, and that led to a fulfilled purpose in their generation.

Ideally, sons should learn from the mantle of their fathers and go on in their lifetime in **double portion** anointing. This is what Gehazi was addressing. This was a reward that would surely satisfy this Shunammite.

5. The reward of the *now* word (v16)

It is vital that business kings create the time to hear and receive **now** words to themselves and their businesses. To operate generationally you have to be able to go the distance and receive instruction or direction that is crucial to ongoing success. Jesus taught the value of the **now** words (rhemas) to us (**Matt 4:4**). He said that we should **live** on the rhema words that proceed from the mouth of God. When we hear them, these spoken now words to our situations are so powerful that not even the authorities of Hades can prevail against what has been spoken. **Now** words release to your situation the spoken intent of God and what He has said will be made good. **(Num 23:19)**

We catch a glimpse of the power of a **now** word in the life of Jacob in **Genesis 30:37-43**. Jacob had labored for his Uncle Laban for 20 years under extreme emotional pressure and deception. He had his salary changed ten times, had to work seven years for the wrong wife and had to bear the costs of any losses, even if he was not to blame. After all this time he had nothing to show for his labour and hard work and would have gone back to his home land empty-handed, had it not been for a rhema word from God.

> **Now Jacob took for himself rods of green poplar and of the almond and chestnut trees, peeled white strips in them, and exposed the white which was in the rods. And the rods which he had peeled,**

**he set before the flocks in the gutters, in
the watering troughs where the flocks
came to drink, so that they should
conceive when they came to drink.** So the
**flocks conceived before the rods, and the
flocks brought forth streaked, speckled,
and spotted.**

(Genesis 30:37-39)

In the context of this story, Laban realized that he had
amassed wealth because of Jacob and that is when
Jacob said, **"...the Lord has blessed you since my
coming. And now, when shall I also provide for my
own house?" (Gen 30:30)** Jacob wanted to leave and
go back to where he had come from with his family and
children and have the opportunity to begin his own
family heritage. Laban wanted him to stay on because
his wealth source was about to depart. So when Jacob
came up with the plan that he would stay on and start
his own flocks from all those who were spotted and
stripped, (basically the unwanted sheep) Laban
accepted the terms. Jacob embraced the **now** word of
God to him **(Gen 30:37-39)** and it changed his whole
financial status.

**Thus the man became exceedingly
prosperous, and had large flocks, female
and male servants, and camels and
donkeys.**

(Genesis 30:43)

**Now Jacob heard the words of Laban's
sons, saying, "Jacob has taken away all
that was our father's, and from what was
our father's he has acquired all
this wealth."**

(Genesis 31:1)

This is an important concept for God's kings to understand. Recovery in business can be attained quickly when you receive the rhema word of God and then obey what God speaks as a **now** word for where you are. Jacob laboured endlessly for 20 years, but only prospered personally when God told him how to grow his own flocks. **(Gen 30:37-39)**

The Shunammite woman was given a rhema word—**a promise of a son**—a reward from God for the way she honoured and served Elisha. God reconnected their generational heritage through this son and established a line of heritage for their future. Being positioned under your man of God has strong possibilities for a king's ongoing success. The potential they have spans into generations.

6. **Confidence when your promise is under threat (v19-20)**

Let us remind ourselves that this son was a promised reward from God. The Shunammite hadn't asked for him. He was given because they had no way of establishing their generational destiny. He was a blessing from God. The child came just when Elisha said he would and the family was overjoyed. Then all of a sudden, things went wrong. He became ill one day in the fields with his father, and shortly after returning home to his mother, he died. **(v20)**

Financial kings must be aware of the strategic plans of the devil that he has shown through the ages. Part of his plan has always been to attack something in its infancy. He would often strike out at a promise when it was still in its formative stages. So when a promise is newly born and it is going to be significant, it is definitely vulnerable to attack. The last thing the devil wants is for it to mature and become fruitful. He has enough headaches to deal with.

We only have to remember in **Matthew 2:13-18** when Joseph and Mary fled to Egypt with the baby Jesus, how Herod had thousands of children killed in an attempt to end the rise of another king that had been born. The devil tried to end the life of Jesus whilst He was still an infant. Also in **Exodus 1**, Pharaoh tried to stem the growth of the people of Israel when it was still a fledgling nation in his land. He ordered the midwives to kill the Hebrew children when they were born. **(v15, 16)**

When her son suddenly died, the Shunammite woman didn't panic or fall apart. She managed to keep her composure because she was confident in the power of her **'now'** word from God. What God had given her as a reward and for a generational purpose, the gates of hell could not prevail against. Although her son had died, she went in search for the one who had given the promise and armed her faith with the declaration, **"It is well." (v23, 26)**

Many ideas and opportunities come to business kings. You have been wired to create wealth. Your purpose is to transfer wealth out of the marketplace into the kingdom. New, creative ideas arrive all the time. Those that they run with have the potential to be hugely successful and a great blessing in kingdom purpose. You need to exercise caution when opportunities are still in infancy. That's the time the enemy likes to strike and cause havoc if he is allowed.

Business kings need to have a similar confidence and stance of faith at what God has birthed for you as the

Shunammite woman displayed in this scripture. You need to be secure in what God has promised and given and then guard it against attack. The devil will attempt to derail it before it matures and manifests what God has designed.

7. Go back to the source (v21, 28)

You will often hear from pulpits, "What you order, you will have to maintain. What God orders, He maintains." What God brings to birth, He will finance and keep productive. That is why it is crucial for financial kings to have the rhema word of God. When you have God's now word for your business, you always have something to fall back on. If the project came from the Lord, He will make sure it will live and operate in success. Sadly, many business projects fail because they are only good ideas—not God's. God's ideas will never fail and when kings operate in His ideas, they can rest in the knowledge that they can always go back to the source and maintain their stability.

The Shunammite woman was incredible. As a mother she felt the turmoil and pain that were brought on by her emotions. She had lost her son when still an infant and yet managed to stay focused on God and what to do next. She had not asked for this gift of a son. He was a reward from God. He came as a blessing to her from the prophet of God. He was the result of the word of the Lord to her. How could this happen? Why would God do this? No, this was not the work of God.

> **"God is not a man, that He should lie, Nor a son of man, that He should repent. Has He said, and will He not do? Or has He spoken, and will He not make it good?"**
> **(Num 23:19)**

40

The Shunammite woman knew that no sickness or disease was going to sneak up on them and rob them of the heritage that God had set in place, or cut short her son's destiny before his time. She was distraught and churning up on the inside and was tested to the highest degree, but she kept her composure. She remained in faithful expectation of a good outcome because she knew her God. She took the child straight to the room of her man of God (Elisha) and laid him on his bed. She took the promise back to God who had given it. She went immediately to her source. **(2 Kings 4:21-25)**

We must expect opposition to the plans and intents of God for our business. God wants you to succeed in your financial kingship. We must understand that the devil, particularly when something is in embryonic stages, will endeavour to send deathblows to it. Sometimes they come at you very hard but you can win and must learn to persevere through those times. Like the Shunammite woman, you have a promise from God. Your business is a means to get you to your destiny and purpose in the Lord. God has promised this opportunity to you and the moment it looks like the enemy has dealt it a deathblow, it is not nearly over. Go back to your source. Remind God of His promise to you and what you are standing on and be in expectation that things will shift in your favour.

8. "Pick up your son" (v36)

I can't think of anything more satisfying in life than when something of immense value to you, which has been lost or taken away, is returned in full working order. Nothing brings more joy than God breaking into your circumstances and affecting them positively through the acts of His kindness and favour. In desperate situations when the evidence has mounted and things look serious, you need to be able to turn somewhere for help. That is why you must have the security of knowing the source of your information.

The Shunammite woman knew exactly what had been told to her and who had said it. She held the fulfillment in her arms. She had a promise from God regarding their family's generational outcome and the evidence to prove that what had been said was on track. When she suddenly had to face the devastating news that this promise was now stolen from her, knowing that God was the source of her **now** word helped her stand firm and act in faith. The Shunammite wasn't disappointed. Her faith, confidence, and expectation of what she knew was from God, was rewarded with the words, **"Pick up your son." (v36)** She went back to her source making a demand on it. God honoured her.

Certain faith actions had to be put in place before this event was a reality. Business kings need to be able to return to the source of their mandate from God. The son in this story is symbolic of the business concept given by God, which had now been attacked by the enemy and left for dead. In **(v33-35)** Elisha acted in a way that helps us find a strategy for similar occurrences:

    a. He shut the door on outside intrusions
    b. He prayed to the Lord
    c. He lay on/over the child
    d. He put his mouth on the child's mouth
    e. He put his eyes on the child's eyes
    f. He put his hands on the child's hands
    g. He repeated the process

Elisha was at war with a spiritual attack against the integrity of God. God is not confused. What He has said will happen! Your business is from God. He gave you the mandate to work it successfully in the purpose He has for it. Your job as His steward of the business is to make sure that it progresses in its field.

When you feel the enemy has drawn a line in the sand against you, go to your source and close the door on outside distractions. Get into prayer with God. Recapture what He said (mouth), what He showed you as the vision (eyes) and what you heard from Him (ears). Declare to the working parts (hands) of the business that they will live and produce. Call in a shift in your circumstances. Believe God for a positive change, new opportunities, new clients and a rush on sales. '**Pick up your son**' that has been given to you. Don't let it die. Stand your ground as a king-in-business and wage good warfare and recover all. Declare **Proverbs 10:22**.

9.   Believing God's prophets (2 Kings 8)

Whatever the time span was between **2 Kings 4-8**, we see this family still honouring and making room for their man of God. Elisha was still in close proximity to them. Time hadn't changed that nor had familiarity crept in and interfered with the respect of his anointing. **(Mark 6:1-5)** This is the secret of great reward.

Elisha was a true general in the army of God and was focused on kingdom purpose on the earth. Like Elijah before him, he was a prophet that could hear from God and what he said from God occurred. When Elijah and Elisha each left this earthly realm, the cry that rang out was, **"My father, my father, the chariot of Israel and its horsemen!" (2 Kings 2:12; 2 Kings 13:14)**

These prophets were the real deal. They were generals in heaven's army and spoke the oracles of God in the earth. Our Shunammite woman made sure she embraced and respected this office and the rewards spanned into their future, touching the generations following their family line. She was positioned in the best place imaginable. If Elisha received word from God or any directional encouragement that was intended for her, she was on hand to receive it. As Elisha heard from the throne room, so did she. This is a practice God's kings-in-business would do well to emulate.

And one day it happened. The Shunammite woman received news and direction that would affect the next seven years of her life and business on their farm:

> **Then Elisha spoke to the woman whose son he had restored to life, saying, "Arise and go, you and your household, and stay wherever you can; for the Lord has called for a famine, and furthermore, it will come upon the land for seven years." So the woman arose and did according to the saying of the man of God, and she went with her household and dwelt in the land of the Philistines seven years.**
>
> **(2 Kings 8:1-2)**

Being in this position—close proximity to the man of God—led her to hear the prophetic word, and then ultimately to prosperity. **"...Believe His prophets, and you shall prosper." (2 Chron 20:20)** The Shunammite woman never wasted any seed trying to get a harvest, nor did she try again after a failed year of planting in hope of recuperating her losses. She knew the famine was to last seven years. She didn't have to go to

44

creditors to help her out after using up her supply of seed, nor was she in danger of losing her land to pay off borrowed debt. Instead she gave her land rest for seven years and used what finance she had to keep herself and family alive whilst she waited out the time living amongst the Philistines.

God's business kings would be in a good place if this type of relationship was more of the norm. Whilst you have to rely on hard work and the skill of the anointing on you, it is a comfort and real benefit to have the added advantage of spiritual direction and confirmation as well. This is KEY to recovery and ongoing success in business. **Pastor John Bevere**, who recently visited South Africa, spoke on **Honour and Rewards** with great effect. One of the ways you honour those in authority over you is to bless them financially, particularly when their gifting and prophetic insights have led to your success in the marketplace. What they can release to you helps to shape your destiny as a king-in-business.

**10.   The reward of reconnecting to the original plan
      (2 Kings 8:1-6)**

The Shunammite left her land at the instruction of the Lord. She obeyed the prophetic word. It wouldn't be unreasonable to think that her reconnecting to her equity would also be of the Lord's doing. After all, God knows the timing of things. The Bible tells us that Jesus is the **"...the author and finisher of our faith..."** **(Heb 12:2)** God was the one responsible for getting the message out to the Shunammite woman to not waste her resources on farming for the next seven years. It would turn out that He would prove to be responsible to return to her what was legally hers as well. God made sure that **favour** and **timing** led her to this place supernaturally and she would be reconnected to her original life purpose.

11. The power of God's timing (2 Kings 8:3-5)

Timing is everything. You can plan the most exciting holiday onboard a cruise, but if you arrive a half an hour after the ship has left its berth, you get to watch sadly as your dream holiday floats away from you. If you are a sportsman, particularly where ball sports are concerned, it is timing and not brute force that places you in a league of your own. Commentators will say, "He just seems to have so much time to see the ball. He makes it look so easy."

As humans we have a tendency to want things done quickly, but may be in danger of having the timing off for the best result. Business kings work at a pace as well because **time is money**; however you must be able to judge the right time to do things. You don't want to get ahead or fall behind.

The Shunammite's timing was absolutely amazing—or should I say, her following the lead of the Holy Spirit at the right time, led her into a miraculous outcome. What she experienced and how she connected to the opportunities God had available is the sort of thing God wants for His business kings in the marketplace. These supernatural connections are what take them to new heights in business success.

> **It came to pass, at the end of seven years
> that the woman returned from the land of
> the Philistines; and she went to make an
> appeal to the king for her house and for
> her land. Then the king talked
> with Gehazi, the servant of the man of**

46

**God, saying, "Tell me, please, all the great
things Elisha has done."**
(2 Kings 8:3-4)

Just as he began to explain how Elisha had restored the
dead son of the Shunammite family to life, she arrived
on the scene, **"...appealing to the king for her house
and for her land." (v5)** Many would try to pass this off
as coincidence. But when God is involved and you are
following His lead, your life and circumstances connect
with the miracles He has placed in your path. You may
feel in the natural that nothing is really different, until
you collide with God's plan and realize just how in
control He is. The power of this timing was
unbelievable. Had the woman come an hour later, or
arrived the day before, she would not have had the
audience that led to her supernatural encounter with the
king. The power of God's timing was everything in this
case.

12. The reward of compensation (2 Kings 8:6)

We have been speaking about the flow of reward that
manifested in the Shunammite woman's life. When she
began by making room for the man of God that was
visiting their area, she had no idea how that act of
kindness and honour of God's prophet, would lead to
events that positioned them as a family for generational
blessing. God made sure that when she arrived in His
perfect timing to speak to the king, all was ready for her
to receive the blessing of a lifetime. Because of her
obedience, God planned for her to be fully compensated
for the seven years she didn't receive an income from
her land; and in addition, had her land and house
restored to their name. The king ordered:

"Restore all that was hers, and all the proceeds of the field from the day that she left the land until now."

(2 Kings 8:6)

God set things in place that would reach into the next generation for them as a family. You must make the effort to be around God and His rhema opportunities for you. You must make a decision to honour the man of God sent into your life. Those who put God first and seek first the kingdom, have these things added to them. Your obedience to God's leading and what He sends to you by way of gifting, will certainly help you in your current dealings as a king-in-business and help you along the road of recovery, so that things can be put in place to strengthen your foothold for the next generation.

One simple decision made very early on in their life as a family, led to dividends going into the next generation.

Chapter Four

GOD'S SYNERGY
FOR GENERATING FINANCE

Now when Abram heard that his brother
was taken captive, he armed his three
hundred and eighteen
trained servants who were born in his
own house, and went in pursuit as far as
Dan.

(Genesis 14:14)

Then Melchizedek king of Salem brought
out bread and wine; he was the priest
of God Most High. And he blessed him
and said: "Blessed be Abram of God Most
High, Possessor of heaven and earth;
And blessed be God Most High, Who has
delivered your enemies into your hand."
And he gave him a tithe of all.

(Genesis 14:18-20)

But Abram said to the king of Sodom,
"I have raised my hand to the Lord, God
Most High, the Possessor of heaven and
earth, (23) that I will take nothing, from a
thread to a sandal strap, and that I will
not take anything that is yours, lest you
should say, 'I have made Abram rich'…"

(Genesis 14:22-23)

THE VALUE OF THE ANCIENT PATHS

There are some things in life that are foundational and crucial to ensure a pattern of success. Why the need to re-invent the wheel? If you stray from these ancient principles that have stood the test of time, you are in danger of opening up pathways that may not be necessary which could lead you off-track and become responsible for contributing to your business downfall. The prophet Jeremiah offered this advice:

> **"Stand in the ways and see,**
> **And ask for the old paths,**
> **where the good way is,**
> **And walk in it;**
> **Then you will find rest for your souls."**
>
> **(Jeremiah 6:16)**

Some things are set in place by God and won't move. Following them, whether a Christian or not, will result in the rewards for which they were established. For example, many different ethnic groups around the world practice the concept of giving and benefit from this biblical promise. This is because God sets this principle eternally. It is established in the **ancient ways** and **pathways**. It is part of the **good way** and those who find it have rest. Any person who is generous and desires to give will reap the benefits of being a giver. God has established the principle, **"Give, and it shall be given to you: good measure, pressed down, shaken together, and running over will be put into your bosom" (Luke 6:38)**. Financial blessing is a plan of God and is one of those **ancient paths** that we should seek to understand. This plan is part of the **old ways** that still work for those who discover them and choose to **walk in them.**

Later on, Jeremiah cautioned the people for failing to honour these ancient paths. They no longer abided in these truths and had moved away from the principles and practices that kept them in relationship with God.

> **"Because My people have forgotten Me,**
> **They have burned incense to worthless**
> **idols.**
> **And they have caused themselves to**
> **stumble in their ways,**
> **From the ancient paths,**
> **To walk in pathways and not on a**
> **highway…"**
> **(Jeremiah 18:15)**

The ancient paths are established, working principles that create highways for us to walk upon. They lead us into experiencing the truths of God's word. They make the difference in us and set us apart from the world. God developed a pathway to achieve financial success for His people a long time ago. He has put in place principles that will produce harvest, increase and recovery of loss, despite the economy. He has released a synergy of gift ministries to create this wealth for His business kings. These **ancient paths** will cause us to **stand** and **see** that what God has built into His principles will increase **rest** for us. So *old* doesn't have to mean *obsolete*. Old doesn't have to mean what the modern world thinks today. With God, old is the wise path to choose. They were there at the foundation. These principles have worked from the beginning. They have eternal value. They are here to work until God says *no more*. They will not cease to work the way God intended them to operate.

> **"While the earth remains,**
> **Seedtime and harvest,**
> **Cold and heat,**

51

Winter and summer,
And day and night
Shall not cease."

(Genesis 8:22)

THE POWER OF THE PROPHET-PRIEST-KING GIFTING

The business king needing recovery and those who are wanting to achieve better results in their business dealings, would do well to consider and entertain the ancient path of the **PROPHET – PRIEST – KING** synergy of breakthrough that God has laid out in His word. Although these individual gifts are each powerful in their own right and able to accomplish incredible breakthroughs in peoples' lives and circumstances, their power is enhanced and magnified when they operate in synergy together. The prophet Samuel and King David operated in this dimension. They were an awesome ministry and unbelievably powerful in their time. Jesus epitomized this synergy to the full extent and nothing could touch Him—not even death—until He chose to lay His life down. This synergy definitely has great prospects for those kings-in-business who embrace and submit to its working methodology, as laid out in the ancient paths. Creating a flow of finance into the church or kingdom is the main function but understand it will be met with fierce opposition. The last thing the devil wants is for the church to prosper and be in a position to fulfill its mandate from God.

The **PROPHET** (when speaking in the financial realm) has the power and authority to create an open heaven where provisions arrive to meet both current and future needs. (Look again at the widow's miracle provision that was released through Elisha in **2 Kings 4:1-7**).

The **PRIEST** (set man/pastor/leader of congregation) has been delegated the authority to speak and activate the power of **BLESSING** in every situation. God commanded the new assembled priesthood just out of Egypt, to **bless** the people of God and gave them a specific way to do this. **(Num 6:22-27)** Also in the book of Deuteronomy, God tells the priests that they were chosen by Him to minister **blessing**. He wanted them to be amongst His people and bless every controversy and assault the people faced, until it settled. The power of **BLESSING** has the ability to create change in the places it has been sent. **(Deut 21:5)**

Using the word BLESS in your prayer has only a limited understanding amongst most western world Christians. But to speak and release BLESSING from the Hebrew understanding has a completely different meaning. The word BLESS carries the added meaning of, *to empower success, to prosper, to favour, to benefit, to add value and to unlock exactly what is suited to the situation.* So when the PRIEST speaks BLESSING to his financial kings, he is anointed to release **creative words of power** that **deposit prophetic seed** to effect change, develop prosperity, favour, and added value to the situation. Instead of having a stagnant, unproductive business, BLESSING helps create what God intends the situation to have. The more God's priests understand how to speak blessing, the more each person's boundaries of received blessing can increase and expand. This is very good for a king-in-business.

When it comes to the business **KING**, he has been given power to create wealth. **(Deut 8:18)** His destiny and mandate from God is to produce wealth. God has given these kings the ability, skill, and anointing to operate successfully in the marketplace. They belong in this arena, just like a fish lives in water. Their success and generous giving rapidly advances the kingdom on the earth.

So when these gifts operate in synergy together **(Prophet-Priest-King)** they release a powerful anointing where they are situated. Results will manifest and progress will be achieved. This synergy is a powerful ancient path.

It is also interesting to note that this synergy was used whenever leaders wanted to restore the image of God or exact a presence of God that the people had wandered away from. For example, in **Haggai 1:1-4**, the temple needed restoring because the image of God through the poor physical state of the temple, did not create the picture that Israel's God was God above all gods Teams of **Prophets-Priests-Kings**, working in synergy, were sent to change that. **(2 Chron 34:8)** In those times, the condition and décor of a temple formulated an opinion in people's minds of the value of the god it was representing. So to the Hebrews, if their temple was in a poor state and run down, it invariably meant that God was not a high priority amongst them.

This concept underlines the importance of having this synergy operating in the body of Christ today. For the church to effectively win the lost and reach its community in a real way, it will take both finance and sensitivity to the Holy Spirit, to achieve it with success. With the witness and value of God diminishing in many nations, we don't want to add to their discontent when they see that the church is always begging for money and can't really afford anything. It becomes too easy for them to have the view, "Why should I belong to a community whose God cannot afford what He stands for?" You may share the feeling that money is not everything, but how can poverty be helpful?

FIRST MENTIONS ARE IMPORTANT

God set this synergy in place way back in the book of **first mentions**. The first real picture of this breakthrough strategy is seen in **Genesis 14:14-23**. Those who discover its value and working ethic find the good way in this ancient path and the release of wealth into the church becomes more accessible. God's business kings need to create and establish a flow of finance into the church. From their generosity, the church will not lack the finance to fulfill the vision of God has given it.

Melchizedek (in the office of a priest) entered the frame **(v 18)** and what transpired was before 'the law' was given. It was not just an Old Testament principle. In Melchizedek's genealogy, he had no beginning or end, and therefore represents the eternal priesthood—spanning both Old and New Testaments. What was given as a strategy to work then will still work today. What Melchizedek demonstrated to Abram was the strategy to stimulate and create a flow of finance from the wealth of the world, into the hands of God's business kings. God used him to reveal a plan that would last for all time, despite challenges that occur in the economy Melchizedek's arrival at that time showed Abram:

1) **PRIESTS** need to go onto their business king's turf. They carry an anointing to bring increase and have an ability to extend trade borders. Priests should set a regular time slot to visit these premises. Priests carry an anointing not only to bless, but also their blessing can settle assaults and attacks from the enemy. **(Deut 21:5)** The blessing a priest carries is able to catapult businesses to higher levels of productivity and success.

2) After being allowed where only kings could go (The King's Valley), Melchizedek called for the bread and wine. **(v18)** He functioned in the capacity of a **PRIEST** and broke bread with Abram. He celebrated communion

with him, reminding Abram who his resource was, and just who he was in relationship with and responsible for all his successes. After his first success in the marketplace, he was immediately reminded of who brought it about. Celebrating communion honours God and reminds us of His covenant. By participating, you symbolically eat and drink the body of Christ—the absolute power of who God is and what He represents. When you are weak, then He is strong. When you are unable to achieve, He is more than able and can do all things. Celebrating communion causes the king-in-business to remain levelheaded, knowing that it's not the next deal that provides for him. It is God who does that. It is God who is his resource.

3) Melchizedek then operated in another **PRIESTLY** function and **BLESSED** Abram. **(v19)** The Hebrew understanding of *to bless* has already been explained, but to have an anointing to release the power to succeed, favour, and prosper; must not be missed. The priest has the ability to address every business controversy and speak to it BLESSINGS so that it could change and become positively affected.

4) After these priestly functions, Melchizedek then affirmed a **PROPHETIC** word previously spoken over Abram. **(v19-20)** Abram was reminded that he would be a possessor in the earth and his enemies would be delivered into his hands.

What happened next was the response of Abram as a business **KING.** He showed his desire to give; to be a conduit of blessing. He immediately gave Melchizedek a

tithe of all his spoil, **(v20)** although Melchizedek did not
even ask for it. Business kings have an ability and skill
level to operate successfully in the marketplace. But when
that skill level is placed together with the priestly and
prophetic anointing, the business king draws to himself a
continual release of blessing and accurate prophetic timing.
The king will have a measure of success from his own
anointing, but when in **synergy** with a **priest** and **prophet**,
his successes go way beyond what he could have imagined.
God needs His business kings to break through in the area
of finances at the level that is good to God, and His level is
always way beyond what we can believe. This synergy
allows the business king to then successfully perform what
he is anointed to do—create wealth and provide freely for
the advancement of God's kingdom on the earth. This is his
mandate. This is his purpose. This is what brings him
fulfillment.

This strategy is an **ancient path**. This is where the **good
way** is found and leads to rest. This is a strategy that must
be re-visited by the church and taken seriously if you are a
business king who needs to recover in business or ensure
ongoing progression. It is an eternal principle established
long before the arguments of whether it was 'law' or not. It
is not governed or affected by marketplace crashes or
uncertain economies. It is a strategy that will work in all
seasons and must become a living practice in the church
once again. It's not an **ancient path** for nothing. It was
introduced to Abram, at the start of his role as a king-in-
business, conquering for God in the marketplace and
having heaps of spoil to show for the efforts.

Business kings would do well to heed this particular
synergy of gift ministries working together. For me this
strategy is very significant. It's a piece of the puzzle God
says to not miss. It will be extremely beneficial and be of
great value in the world of finance. This is the **good way**

that we must re-discover, for it has the measure over the stresses that arrive in the world's financial realm. Even if the systems of the world fail dismally, they don't dictate or determine what God is able to do. For example:

1) How does water appear in the ditches dug in the valley, when there was no rain? **(2 Kings 3:17)**

2) How does an army flee in terror from another army that they hear advancing but do not see? **(2 Kings 7:6)**

3) How does a widow pay off her debts and end up having a pension fund for the rest of her life, when all she had was a little jar of oil in her house? **(2 Kings 4:1-7)**

4) How do the widow's sons get rescued at the 11th hour from the creditors when all seemed hopeless? **(2 Kings 4:1-7)**

These miracles work because God operates outside of our natural boxes. The supernatural is not strange to Him. God is still more than **"...able to do exceedingly abundantly above all that we ask or think, according to the power that works in us." (Eph 3:20)** The world banks or monetary systems don't have what God has put in us. What we have is a supernatural ability of God to succeed despite natural market indicators. *Therefore, we are not subject to the world and its intentions.* We have God's **ancient paths** working out the **good way** for us. We are in this world but not of it. This becomes a powerful testimony for God. His ancient paths still work and show us the good way. Time to re-look at the SYNERGY and miraculous power that is generated when the 'gift' ministries of PROPHET - PRIEST – KING operate in kingdom purpose.

Chapter Five

REMEMBERING THE WORKS OF GOD

Trust in the Lord, and do good;
Dwell in the land, and feed on His
faithfulness.
Delight yourself also in the Lord,
And He shall give you the desires of
your heart.

(Psalm 37:3-4)

The children of
Ephraim, being armed and carrying
bows,
Turned back in the day of battle.
They did not keep the covenant of God;
They refused to walk in His law,
And forgot His works
And His wonders that He had shown
them.

(Psalm 78:9-11)

REMAIN FAITHFUL

One of the answers to recovery in business is to realize that when you fail or go through tough economic times, it may not be just you feeling the pinch. Markets are uncertain regularly and economic collapses are a reality—creating undue pressure on business. The whole spectrum of banks, governments, and high corporate business can also be affected and when interest rates shoot up, cost of living becomes incredible, and people spending money slows to a minimum. Being able to get cash flow becomes very difficult and if the season persists, it is not long before staff members are laid off and businesses downsize. People are left reeling and in a state of panic and some are forced to sell way below market value or just close down.

God's kings-in-business also feel the same pressure but don't need to experience what is happening to others. They have a recovery plan and an ongoing success strategy that requires faith and a focusing of the mind on the promises of God. God's word says, **"You will keep him in perfect peace, whose mind is stayed on You…" (Isa 26:3)** God has provided a strategy for you to follow that will help you through the same dangers that others experience. Your hope is in Him. God is the resource of your business and knows how to keep it afloat even in difficult economic times. God taught us that we are in this world but not of it. Whilst we are affected by what happens and feel the pressure it creates, we belong to God's kingdom that is governed by another set of laws.

How was Isaac able to produce a hundred-fold return from his land in the midst of a severe drought? **(Gen 26:1-12) God told him to do it** is the simple answer. God was not moved or restricted by the famine. He moved despite it and will do the same for His kings in recessions, crashed markets, and tough economic times. His laws are way above anything the world is caught up in and so we can rest in the understanding that we are on God's economic plan of sustainability and fruitfulness provided we have direction from God.

God's kings must choose to remain faithful to His economic strategies and financial principles, because they are unaffected by what the world suffers. They will show profit and success at the end of the day, but it will require resilience and a steadfastness to keep these financial laws of God's kingdom in the face of the collapses and devastation around them. God wants to crown each year with success. He wants to visit your business and enrich it and water the ridges and furrows until they are smooth and able to produce:

> **You visit the earth and water it,**
> **You greatly enrich it;**
> **The river of God is full of water;**
> **You provide their grain,**
> **For so You have prepared it.**
> **You water its ridges abundantly,**
> **You settle its furrows;**
> **You make it soft with showers,**
> **You bless its growth.**
> **You crown the year with Your goodness,**
> **And Your paths drip with abundance.**
>
> **(Psalm 65:9-11)**

Psalm 37:3-4 (see the beginning of this chapter) offers sound advice on how to act when business is affected by economic strains:

1. **Trust (v3)**

Trusting God is not negotiable. You have to trust God and not lean on your own understanding. Your strength is not on trusting in horses and chariots **(Ps 20:7)** or the next deal on the horizon. You are not likely to get every deal you want. You will suffer many let downs, but as long as you keep in mind that God's promises are always "YES" and "AMEN" in Him, and keep moving towards His plan, you show trust and that is what He wants to see. Business is always subject to change and has many twists and turns that you do not necessarily expect. People outside of God can be ruled by greed and all levels of carnality and these people are your counter-parts in the marketplace and capable of anything that may not help you. They are not reliable, nor can they be depended upon. God alone is the one who is trustworthy. He alone has your best interests at heart. Keep trying and do your best to honour God and your trust will be rewarded.

2.   Dwell in the land (v3)

Become rooted where God has sent you. Don't be in a hurry to move on. The land God has set aside for you is a good land **(Deut 8:7)** and has everything needed to help you succeed. Whatever God authenticates, He authorizes. He takes responsibility for what He tells you to do or where He wants you to go. He always watches over His Word to perform it. **(Jer 1:12)** You will operate under an umbrella of success and prosper in what you do if you dwell where God has earmarked for you. Isaac in **Genesis 26:3** was asked to **"Dwell in this land…"** where he was. Even though there was a destructive famine about, and it made perfect sense to go down to Egypt like everyone else, he did what God asked of him and was rewarded with a hundred-fold return in that year. **(Gen 26:12)**

God's economic plan will produce even when in the natural, it shouldn't. Dwell in the land God has given you. Despite what it looks like currently, it is laden with gold that will make you a financial king for God. Let Him make it all He has seen for you. Dwell in your given land of milk and honey!

3. Do good (v3)

Financial crunches tempt us to behave in ways not conducive to kingdom governance. They have a tendency to cause panic and revert us back to survival mode. This is what Gideon did. He made a small survival loaf of bread daily to feed his family that he had threshed in a winepress the night before. Too much survival thinking creates a *just enough* mindset. Meanwhile God showed him the size of the loaf He was thinking about under the same circumstances. **(Judges 7:13)**

When the pressure is on in business we don't necessarily need to downsize or close up shop. We may not feel we can give as we should, and yes, we will be tempted to hold back the tithe until a more appropriate time and that is exactly what the devil wants from us. No! Don't be caught up in his mind games. God says to **do good.** Do what is right. Act financially in what is the right way to act. No matter what the circumstances, keep doing what is right with the financial governance of God. His economic strategies are tried and tested and proven reliable in these very waters! He establishes ways where there are no ways. He causes breakthrough like a flood of water where it doesn't seem possible. **"Is anything too hard for the Lord?" (Gen 18:14)** Your obedience shows your faithfulness to invest and believe in God's strategies. They cannot fail!

Always practice honouring God first. This has the promise of **"…all these things shall be added to you." (Matt 6:33)** Be mindful of God and not the things we think we need and the rest will naturally arrive. What you give away and not what you keep is the only thing that can be multiplied. This is what Jesus taught when He multiplied the little food they had to feed a large crowd. **(Luke 9:16)** In tough times we are challenged to hold on to our money. It seems the sensible thing to do. But increase can only come from God's principles of supply when you yield in obedience in the face of uncertainty. God uses what you release, not what you keep.

4.   Feed on His faithfulness (v3)

This is absolutely vital to ongoing business success or recovery from a business slump. We should be living on every rhema word that proceeds from the mouth of God. **(Matt 4:4)** These **now** words keep us safe from the prevailing attacks of the enemy. These promises from God will cause us to withstand the lethal desires of the devil, who has no power against these spoken words. They come from the mouth of God. Whatever God has said will be the result.

Whenever a financial king is challenged by lack, fear, dried up cash flow, or even clients not visiting your business as you expect, one of the most positive things he can do is to **feed on God's faithfulness.** The devil's temptation is to get us considering how bad things are and not how capable God is. It is time to reflect on what God has spoken as a rhema to your situation. These now words cannot be stopped. It is also a time to reflect on past situations that were seriously threatening, and how God helped you turn things around in those bleak times. These memories create for us the thinking; *all things are indeed possible with God.* What God has done previously, He is able to do again. God never changes. He is always the same. **(Heb 13:8)** This is very helpful when your mind and emotions want to run away with you and panic desires to set in. The fact that God cannot lie to you, or change the way He operates, is so comforting to remember.

Feeding on the faithfulness of God will help keep alive your hope and faith expectation as these are resources that stimulate and create change.

REMEMBER THE WORKS OF GOD

Reading through **Psalm 78** you cannot fail to pick up the value God placed on **not forgetting the works of God.** This was also the responsibility of fathers to ensure these understandings were handed down through the generations. **(v3-8)** Those that were still to be born had two major things to grasp:

1) The children could set their hope on God **(v7)**
2) They should not forget the works of God **(v7)**

Despite these desires of God for His people, and the teaching of father figures, **"The children of Ephraim, being armed and carrying bows, Turned back in the day of battle." (v9)** This is an action God's kings-in-business should avoid. The day of battle may be hard, even brutal, but it must be faced head-on. If you do nothing, no man's land prevails. The promise of Israel's promised land was a reality, but Joshua still had to conquer all the ruling kings that opposed their inheritance. Caleb's mountain was his, but he still had to fight for it. There is no victory without the taste of battle. It is the same in the financial arena. There will be a battle for your sustainability and success, but you are armed and fortified for the fight. The land is yours. The spoil in your land has your name on it. You have to retrieve it, despite the harshness of the economy and the people opposing you. The men of Ephraim failed in three areas:

1) They did not keep the covenant of God **(v10)**

2) They refused to walk in His law **(v10)**

3) They forgot His works and His wonders **(v11)**

Business kings will prosper when they remember and understand the covenant they have with God and all that it entails. Choosing to walk and abide in God's financial principles that are laid out for your success in the marketplace is the right option to adopt. Refusing to follow or obey these principles makes no sense. God needs His business kings to prosper in the financial arena so that their generosity will advance His kingdom on the earth. Remembering the great feats of God and how He has broken through before is a faith builder that helps you win battle after battle. Ephraim should have remembered:

1) The ten plagues sent by God to soften Pharaoh's heart so Israel could be freed from slavery in Egypt.

2) How God arranged for them to not leave financially strapped and impoverished as a nation; how God caused them to leave with given Egyptian wealth to start their new life in the Promised Land.

3) That God used Moses to divide the Red Sea for Israel and make a path for them to walk to freedom on dry land but used the same passage to drown their pursuers.

4) The cloud and pillar of fire that God sent to lead and protect them.

5) How God opened rocks to give them water in the desert.

6) That God sent them meat in the desert.

Feeding on these memories and on God's faithfulness might just have made the difference to them turning away on the day of battle. They would have remembered that no matter what lay ahead, it was no match for God who was with them.

Every battle has to be faced. It has to be engaged. Tough economic times, uncertain markets, and dry seasons are all par for the course. They have to be encountered and faced. Keep in mind: **"...with God, all things are possible" (Matt 19:26)**, and **"...If God is for us, who can be against us?" (Rom 8:31)** Ephraim was armed with bows and weaponry for their survival and victory in battle. They were equipped to win, but failed because they forgot the keynotes of covenant, obedience, and faith in God.

You as a business king for God have been selected by God to operate in the financial marketplace. You are primed to succeed and armed with skill, anointing, and God's principles to make you a sensational success. You also have the revelatory strategy and synergy that Prophet – Priest – business King produces.

LIMITING GOD

> **Yes, again and again they tempted God,**
> **And limited the Holy One of Israel.**
> **They did not remember His power:**
> **The day when He redeemed them from**
> **the enemy...**
> **(Psalm 78:41-42)**

The saddest behaviour God has often had to deal with in His children is unbelief in His ability. We see so many examples of His people limiting what God is capable of doing. Yet He is the Mighty One, the One who is more than enough for any occasion. We must understand that God is not restricted by what limits us. He has the way to provide breakthrough for the impossible:

1) The widow in **1 Kings 17:8-16** was contemplating her last meal. God showed up by sending Elijah and revealed that her limitations were His opportunities.

2) When Gideon limited his family to a survival loaf of bread, God showed him the size of loaf that He was thinking about. **(Judges 7:13-14)**

3) Even when gravity pulls an axe-head to the bottom of a river, it is unable to limit God. He can make it float upstream. **(2 Kings 6:6)**

4) God is not limited by famine, either—He caused Isaac to reap a hundred fold when he sowed in famine. **(Gen 26:12)**

These examples of our limitations being God's opportunities cannot be exhausted. The Bible abounds with them. God always has a solution and a way where we can't see one. In difficult economic times God's kings should not act as those with no hope. Instead they should trust, remember His covenant, remember the works of God and feed on His faithfulness. They should take to heart that God had a **ram-in-the-bush** for Abraham when he needed it. **(Gen 22:13)** Abraham had no idea that God had already provided this solution. God alone is our resource and our sole provider and should never be limited by our circumstances and natural thinking.

There has not yet been born a situation that God cannot solve. He is our unlimited God. He is the great **I AM** in every circumstance. The more successful we become at removing our limitations of Him, the more we will see Him at work.

Chapter Six

AN OPEN HEAVEN

**Then Elisha said, "Hear the word of
the Lord. Thus says the Lord: 'Tomorrow
about this time a seah of fine flour shall
be sold for a shekel, and two seahs of
barley for a shekel, at the gate of
Samaria.'"
So an officer on whose hand the king
leaned answered the man of God and
said, "Look, if the Lord would make
windows in heaven, could this thing be?"
And he said, "In fact, you shall see it with
your eyes, but you shall not eat of it."**

(2 Kings 7:1-2)

OUR IMPOSSIBILITIES ARE GOD'S OPPORTUNITIES

Many times in our business lives we face situations we
know are difficult to recover from, and to find a way to
move forward just seems impossible. It's the place where
business kings get to where they cannot see an escape
route. They have hit a wall. A key in assisting recovery
here is to get to the place where you believe God has a plan
that you haven't seen as yet, similar to Abraham's **ram in
the bush** example. His answer was always there, just not
visual. We spend so much time rehearsing why things

69

won't change or what history has proven in the past, but very little time considering what God can do. What is **impossible** to us is always an **opportunity** for God to be glorified. HE knows the way forward.

In **2 Kings 7**, there was a famine that left the city reeling in its wake. It was so severe that people were entering into cannibalism and fighting over donkeys' heads just to keep themselves alive. Even the lepers waiting for scraps at their place at the bottom of the city's walls decided to pack up and take their chances with the enemy actually besieging the city. These circumstances had persisted for quite some time so that the people had lost hope of anything-different occurring. The prevailing situation had conditioned them to believe that things were here to stay.

This was the moment Elisha arrived and presented the Word of the Lord that was designed to build faith for expectant change.

Difficult situations are not foreign in biblical stories. For example:

1) Was it possible for someone to be raised from the dead and then appear in the flesh after being in a tomb for three days? **(Luke 24)**
2) Could the dry bones in Ezekiel's valley really live again? **(Ezekiel 37)**
3) Could a donkey really talk to its master, Balaam? **(Numbers 22)**
4) Could the walk of four lepers really sound like a whole army on the march? **(2 Kings 7)**
5) Could a woman whose sons were ransom for her husband's debts really pay the whole debt and live off the rest from just a small bottle of oil? **(2 Kings 4)**

70

6) Could a stick in a man's hand really divide the sea to make a pathway for freedom? **(Exodus 14)**

7) Could a widow be saved from the pangs of death after first giving a portion of her last meal to a prophet of God? **(1 Kings 17)**

These are just a few of the stories that are seen through the windows of heaven that mark the ongoing acts of God in our helpless and desperate situations. When God sends a Word to you like He did here through Elisha, regardless of what the natural picture looks like, it would be wise to trust what God is saying. He has insight that you don't. He can open up a window of opportunity into your impossibility just as easy as that! His windows open over your life and what is impossible to you falls through into your circumstances. He can and does do this. He is God.

In **2 Kings 7**, there was the promise of abundant food at a specific time when in the current crisis it just didn't seem plausible. God has windows in heaven ready to open in your impossible circumstances.

In **Genesis 16**, Hagar, Sarah's help, discovered this reality when she was abandoned and alone in the desert with a very uncertain future staring down at her. She had nowhere to go and was in a desperate place when suddenly an angel of the Lord appeared and spoke God's advice and plans for her. Where she thought she was completely alone, a window of heaven opened over her, and God's comfort and direction flooded and engulfed her with hope, purpose, and a solution for her current position. As a memorial of that occasion, Hagar named the well, **"Beer Lahai Roi," (Gen 16:14)** which means, **"the well of the One who lives and sees me."**

God lives in our circumstances as well. He sees where we are. He has a window in heaven ready to open over us when things seem hopelessly impossible.

THE WISDOM OF THE DAY IS NOT ALWAYS RIGHT

The king was also very perplexed about the outcome the siege was having on the city and on the behavior of its citizens. An officer, whose hand supported the king as he walked around, **(2 Kings 7:2)** held a prestigious position. He was privy to the highest counsel and decision-making team in the city. There was not much discussed that he wasn't aware of. He would have heard the discussions that went on between the king and his leaders regarding their situation and realized that they had accepted there was no hope for them. They had exhausted every possible means of being saved. So when Elisha presented a shift in their position and prophesied a solution—an abundance of food at a certain time—this officer responded with utter disbelief. It just was not possible. For his outburst against the word of the Lord, he was told that he would see the solution with his own eyes but would not get to partake of it. **(2 Kings 7:2)**

Business kings need to be careful whose hands they lean on. Sometimes the wisdom from the best quarters in town can be very wrong. People in the know in the natural are no match for the windows of heaven that God can open up over your circumstances. Always consider what God can do. Always be influenced by the word of God and the prophetic word He sends your way. When a prophet speaks, God's windows have a way of opening up just when you need them to.

SEE BEYOND THE INEVITABLE

A huge factor for any business king, whether he needs to progress further or find a way to recover, is to keep alive the thought that God has called him into financial kingship. God has his best interest at heart and has hope for him when things seem hopeless. Kings need to work hard at keeping their faith expectancy alive and well. Trust God for **His inevitable providence**—He has the ability to open up the windows of heaven and pour into your circumstances amazing provision. Reaching a difficult place does not mean necessarily the end is in sight. God always sees what we can't and knows when to open the windows of His provision. It's always advisable to stay in faith and expectancy. These are catalysts that keep open the windows and what God has said will always materialize.

This is similar to what Elisha tried to explain to his servant in **2 Kings 6:13-17**. What the servant couldn't see, Elisha was seeing supernaturally. Elisha saw angels and the chariots of heaven's army in ascendancy over the Syrian forces that were surrounding them, and knew then that he and his servant were protected from harm. God was showing him the real picture. What we see naturally and form opinions upon is often how the enemy wants us to respond. God showed here that for every natural picture there was a spiritual one as well. We may not always see it, but must start believing in these inevitable providences of God.

Heaven is completely aware of the goings-on around your business circumstances. There are millions of angels ready to be dispatched to give you the upper hand at any one moment. There are windows of blessing that can be opened to you where things seem impossible. There are angelic beings under the command of the **Lord of Hosts** ready to be loosed to fight on your behalf. We must learn to see the inevitable that is with God. It's never over until God says it is. HE can drop a word or promise into your hopelessness and make it go away as if it never existed.

What this story teaches, is that with God all things are possible. The windows of heaven's goodness can and do open over your impossibilities. Are you more moved by the knowledge of experts (and they have their place) than by the ability of God in your circumstances? Your sensitivity to be able to hear God is paramount to your rescue as well as the value you personally attach to the Prophetic? It was a Prophet of God that revealed the final outcome in this scenario. Believing God's prophets leads to you prospering. **(2 Chron 20:20)**

Chapter Seven

CREATING MOVEMENT

Now there were four leprous men at the
entrance of the gate; and they said to one
another, "Why are we sitting here until
we die? If we say, 'We will enter the city,'
the famine is in the city, and we shall die
there. And if we sit here, we die also. Now
therefore, come, let us surrender to
the army of the Syrians. If they keep us
alive, we shall live; and if they kill us, we
shall only die." And they rose at twilight
to go to the camp of the Syrians; and
when they had come to the outskirts of
the Syrian camp, to their surprise no
one was there. For the Lord had caused
the army of the Syrians to hear the noise
of chariots and the noise of horses—the
noise of a great army; so they said to one
another, "Look, the king of Israel has
hired against us the kings of the Hittites
and the kings of the Egyptians to attack
us!" Therefore they arose and fled at
twilight, and left the camp intact—their
tents, their horses, and their donkeys—
and they fled for their lives.

(2 Kings 7:3-7)

MOVEMENT CREATES OPPORTUNITY

A river, depending on its size, is normally a picture of life and activity. As it flows over grasslands and savannas, through valleys, and from mountain regions to the sea, it provides a life source for animals, industry, farmers, and even residences. Cities and towns tend to grow up around rivers, because they have found ways to harness its flow and turn it into a power source that would benefit them in some way. They use it to drive turbines that generate power, or they direct its path down canals to provide a transport source or use it for irrigation for farmers. The point is that where there is water there is life, and where there is a source of water, there is **movement**. That is why when water flows into a place where there is no outlet it usually dies by silting up and becoming stagnant. It has to move.

It is that way in business as well. Unless **movement** surrounds your business it stands to be in danger of becoming stagnant. You are normally in business because the product you have is required by various types of consumers and their interest and buying power keeps you liquid and in cash flow. The moment this flow is stopped or hindered, the business life becomes threatened. Movement is an absolutely crucial element in our businesses and Christian lives as well.

MAINTAIN MOVEMENT

Most CEOs of companies would have a series of graphs and statistics, either on display or on their computers, dissecting every angle of their trade actions. This is to give a visual presentation of how effectively they are doing in the marketplace and the balance between production and sales. They must have their fingers on that pulse, because if they let things just flow and it starts heading where it shouldn't, they will be in trouble soon enough. The moment a CEO sees the demand for his product is slowing down, he has to make an assessment and find a solution quickly. He may have to beef up his marketing strategy or see why the sales team is missing their mark. But he has to act. Sales means life for the company and he has to ensure that there is movement in every sector of the company in order to meet their targets.

Targets and goals are set and incentives create stimulation for **movement** of product. Many companies have salesmen of the year bonuses, which are really worthwhile, and that helps to create consistent movement of sales. You never just sit back and expect things to happen just because you have a good trade name or you have been around for a while. You are always scrutinizing where you are in relation to your set targets and goals. You have to maintain movement, or the company will grind to a halt.

MOVE EVEN IF IT'S CUMBERSOME

The four lepers were in serious trouble in our story. They were not allowed to be in public mixing with normal, healthy people, and therefore had to rely on the charity and giving of the people in the city (from a distance) to keep them alive and supported. In this case, with the city under siege, they waited at the bottom of the city walls for people to lower baskets of food down to them. The famine was severe and the siege that was mounted by the Syrians was beginning to have serious effect. The people in the city were under extreme pressure to find food and in some cases there were acts of cannibalism. Donkeys' heads were at a high price as well. This made the lepers' situation even more precarious, as they were fast approaching the bottom of the food chain list—something had to change for them and it needed to be done quickly.

The lepers made a very important discovery at that time. It's amazing how often a pressure situation leads to a solution being discovered. One of the lepers got up and addressed their problem by saying, **"Why are we sitting here until we die?" (v3)**, or *why are we just waiting around for the inevitable? The people we have been relying on can obviously no longer help us. Let's do something.* They knew that whether they chose to enter the city or sit where they were, the outcome would be the same: death **(v4)** Surrendering to the Syrians was the last option, and the only one that offered a glimmer of hope, **"If they keep us alive we shall live; and if they kill us we shall only die." (v4)**

In the natural it was a catch-22 situation. If they stayed where they were and the siege persisted, they would certainly die. If they went over to the Syrians, they had a fifty percent chance of staying alive. The miracle that resulted came from their decision to **move** from their current position. It is always a good idea to give God something to work with. As they moved from where they were and embraced the unknown and the uncertain, this was the catalyst God needed to work His miraculous. As soon as they created movement, God moved as well. God used the steps of the lepers and **"...caused the army of the Syrians to hear the noise of chariots and the noise of horses–the noise of a great army..." (v6)** This took the Syrians by complete surprise and they fled in great haste for their lives, leaving all their resources and food for Israel to plunder. Thus the word of Elisha was fulfilled. **(2 Kings 7:1)** Of all the people, nobles, and soldiers in the city, God used the steps of four lepers to end the siege that brought such devastation. God used their **movement** to establish how He would move.

This is what Elisha had prophesied to the people. He promised that 'tomorrow about this time' the people will have some food. **(v1)** He did not say that the lepers would pave the way. He spoke by the Spirit of God that food would arrive. But here is a lesson that all business kings should learn: When you hear the rhema word of God (the now spoken word) or receive a word from a prophet that is a confirmation to your spirit, **movement** is what God wants to see next. You are the one that initiates the change of circumstances. You are able to make things happen. God needs you to create the flow of movement and He will do the rest. The prophet Isaiah taught us that when things are barren, we should **SING** as if they weren't. **(Isa 54:1)** He added that when things were tight and there was no potential for growth, that we should then enlarge our tents, lengthen our cords, strengthen our stakes, and do not spare. **(Isa 54:2)**

You have to make it happen. You have to create movement so God has something to work with. He needs to see your faith in action. Why sit around waiting to go under or implode? Even if you feel the least likely to initiate anything (like a leper), still create movement because God is not a respecter of persons. He is able to arrange a lifeline, even from unexpected sources. (An enemy camp) Nothing can stand in the way of God pouring out His blessing over your business, except your inaction. Make sure to do the following:

1) Monitor the statistics of your business, and have your finger is on the pulse of it. If you notice things are not doing well, don't sit back and wait for something to happen. Investigate and create movement for God to add something supernatural.

2) Honour the prophetic word, because you will prosper as a result of your obedience. **(2 Chron 20:20)**

3) Tithe from your business, not just your salary. Your business needs to have the devourer kept at bay as well. **(Mal 3:11)**
4) Give generously to the poor. As you preserve them, God will do so in kind for you.
5) Sow seed so you can inherit God's financial harvests.

As much as you create movement for God to do something supernatural in your business, kings-in-business must honour God's economic strategies despite circumstances. Obedience to these principles will always stimulate a reaction from God. When you MOVE to obey, God will MOVE to create. God will always honour His word and those who operate on His financial principles will always bring to them themselves the movement of His blessing despite the circumstances. God is not restricted by what happens in our economy. We must show what we believe by how we respond to our situations. Remember what James said:

> **Thus also faith by itself, if it does not have works, is dead.**
> **But someone will say, "You have faith, and I have works." Show me your faith without your works, and I will show you my faith by my works.**
> **(James 2:17)**

Movement is the key to your recovery. What can you do to create it in your circumstances? Even if it feels cumbersome (I'm sure the lepers' condition restricted their movement), we should stimulate some form of movement to give God something of faith to work from. God longs to see our faith in action. All things are possible with God. Even if you feel that the movement you can create is really a paltry effort, God will use it to change things. Jesus didn't need a whole line of supply trucks to feed the 5000 men (probably closer to 20000 people all in all). He accepted a little boy's lunch and BLESSED it to multiply. He does not change. He is the same yesterday, today and forever. You have the same opportunity to experience the goodness of God.

Chapter Eight

HELP FROM UNEXPECTED QUARTERS

Now Naaman, commander of the army of
the king of Syria, was a great and
honorable man in the eyes of his master,
because by him the Lord had given
victory to Syria. He was also a mighty
man of valor, but a leper. And the Syrians
had gone out on raids, and had brought
back captive a young girl from the land of
Israel. She waited on Naaman's
wife. Then she said to her mistress, "If
only my master were with the prophet
who is in Samaria! For he would heal him
of his leprosy." And Naaman went in and
told his master, saying, "Thus and thus
said the girl who is from the land of
Israel."
Then the king of Syria said, "Go now, and
I will send a letter to the king of Israel."
So he departed and took with him ten
talents of silver, six thousand shekels of
gold, and ten changes of clothing.

(2 Kings 5:1-5)

COMPANIES SHOULD HEAR THE IDEAS OF THE INSIGNIFICANT

Naaman was an influential person in Syria. In fact, he was the commander of the army **(v1)** and one of the hands on which the king leaned. According the king of Syria, Naaman was a great and honourable man, mighty in valour and one who had brought victory to their nation on numerous occasions. His level of commitment to Syria was duly noted and as a result, he climbed the ladder of success very quickly. In Naaman's case, the words of a young captive Israeli girl who served in his house were the seed that led to the miracle that provided his healing. She mentioned that there was prophet from home that would heal his leprosy. We will discover shortly that even the people at the top of the scale need the small, mundane, and insignificant ones placed strategically within their reach or in close proximity.

Large companies in our communities that have stood the test of time are symbols of business success today. They may have started in very humble beginnings, where the directors were little known, but nevertheless grew because of their winning formula. They were just a dream at one stage but through wisdom and good business sense they grew and became household names in the marketplace. Today they are powerful operations, influential and probably the first choice of consumers. Their directors come to work today a lot differently than when they first started—then they weren't known, but today many people know of them. In former years they were hoping their business would be noticed, and today they rule their piece of the land God has given them. So keep in mind that even the big guys were little guys at some stage.
Just because you may not be at the same level as someone else or reached the heights they have managed to do, does not mean that you are insignificant and that what you have

to say is not good enough. Big breakthroughs often come from lesser sources. Those in places of authority need to heed the gifts in those around them, even when they are not at your place of seniority. Being little in value or influence from the world's perspective does not measure up on God's scales. Those who are anointed of God but are not yet at the heights of their potential success, are opportunities just waiting to be connected to the right source. They have what it takes to be as successful as anyone else.

Naaman was a powerful and important man in his nation. Only the highest officials were his regular companions. What would it do to his reputation if people got to hear that he was following the advice of an unknown slave girl, from another nation? Would the king still want to lean on his hand and count on his council and military advice? God always speaks to us through the still small voice, the rhema word or the now spoken word in our situation. These rhemas, Jesus taught us from **Matthew 4:1-4**, are revelatory in nature and proceed from the mouth of God. They are to be lived on, more than the staple diet of bread! They have the power to stop Satan in his tracks—so if that 'now' word came from a slave in your own house, should her position nullify the truth of what God was saying to Naaman? Certainly not! Released by the spirit, they are more powerful and meaningful than the words relayed by the natural ability of your CEO.

Naaman's breakthrough against leprosy came because he dared to faithfully hear what a smaller, less influential person had to say about God. He latched on to the hope it produced, and he pursued it. Breakthrough ideas don't always arrive from the elite of society. There is truth in hanging around those who are successful, but don't turn away from those 'little' people who haven't been recognized as yet.

LITTLE KNOWN RIVERS

Never despise the little things. Naaman was a man that was used to dealing in high society life. His social standing created that platform. He had become used to dealing with the best qualified people in top circles. As a result, when he approached Elisha, the prophet of God, for his healing, he was put off that Elisha told him to go and bathe in a bitty, struggling river in Israel. Didn't this prophet know that the Abanah and Pharpar rivers of Damascus were far superior rivers than anything in Israel? What could an excuse for a river do for him when he had the waters of Damascus at his disposal? **(2 Kings 5:12)** It was here that Naaman nearly lost the healing God wanted him to have. He measured his stature and importance against the river that had been designated to help him and saw it unworthy of his obedience. He really wanted a river of might and substance.

God wants your obedience rather than the view you attach to the profile you have of yourself. Kings-in-business need to be prepared to listen to God's instructions, regardless of whether they are considered menial when compared to what the popular word is in the marketplace right now. Pursuing an ordinary task should be just as relevant as pursuing one of greater significance. It's not the significance of the instrument that determines the blessing. Many companies in the past have fallen short of their mark having failed to bathe in the rivers of God's choice. Choosing those 'rivers' as a source of income appears to be not worth the effort. Natural tendencies and what the company has always done in the past don't necessarily take it to breakthrough. Ongoing success and recovery is determined by the still, small voice of God. And it may just come from someone we consider not our equal!

God changed Naaman's circumstances because his need was greater than his pride or social standing. When he heard the word of hope through one who was a servant in his household, he responded. His faith became EXPECTANT. He went in search of the one who was a prophet from the God of Israel and one who had the testimony of God's power to heal. Not only did he get healed, but he met the God of Israel through Elisha and returned with two mules' loads of Israel's soil, to remind him of his experience. He wanted a piece of what happened in Israel with him at all times. He wanted it known that the gods of Syria were not anything like the God of Israel. **(2 Kings 5:15-17)**

THE LITTLE BOY'S FISH

One of the greatest miracles recorded in the Bible is the feeding of the 5,000 men (not counting the women and children) where the lunch of a little boy (two fish and five small loaves) was used to bless and sustain the multitude. **(Matthew 14:13-21)** Thousands sat and listened to Jesus and before He sent them home He wanted to feed them. Jesus wasn't intimidated by the inadequate size of the lunch He had to work with. He knew what God could do when blessing was spoken over something. All God needs is evidence of a little faith to work massive changes in our lives and circumstances.

As you hear the still, small voice of God in your business, obey without question. Even if it looks insignificant, do what God says. The result will be miraculous, and like Naaman, you will always have a piece of evidence to prove how God came through for you. Take note of the little you have and offer it to God. God desires something to work with, even if it is ridiculously undersized. A little with Him goes a long way. Resist making the mistake of despising small beginnings. **(Zech 4:10)**

In God's eyes, the little people count just as much as those who have made it already in this world's system. You may be a little business compared to others, but your revelation on how God does things in the financial realm comes to you in a God-sized package. It will ultimately lead to your healing in business. Also keep an ear out for those in your company who are not of any stature as yet. They have ideas and thoughts that may just be an answer for where you are currently stationed.

Chapter Nine

SIMPLE ANSWERS FOR TOUGH PLACES

> **Then he went and sent to Jehoshaphat**
> **king of Judah, saying, "The king of Moab**
> **has rebelled against me. Will you go with**
> **me to fight against Moab?"**
> **And he said, "I will go up; I am as**
> **you are, my people as your people, my**
> **horses as your horses." Then he said,**
> **"Which way shall we go up?"**
> **And he answered, "By way of the**
> **Wilderness of Edom."**
> **So the king of Israel went with the king of**
> **Judah and the king of Edom, and they**
> **marched on that roundabout route seven**
> **days; and there was no water for the**
> **army, nor for the animals that followed**
> **them.**

> **(2 Kings 3:7-9)**

THE DANGER OF EMOTIONAL ATTRACTIONS

Jehoshaphat was king of Judah and known to be a follower
of God. When Israel came under the threat of Moab,
Jehoshaphat joined forces with the King of Israel and the
King of Edom in order to counter the threat. Ahab was king
of Israel, and together with his wife, Jezebel, was in direct
opposition to the Lord. They were both Baal worshippers

and persecutors of God's prophets. Through an alliance of marriage, Jehoshaphat felt obliged to help Ahab at his point of need. In so doing, he allowed himself to be yoked with two other kings, known to oppose the God he served.

This decision nearly cost them for a number of reasons:
1) Jehoshaphat was unequally yoked in this arrangement. He was subject to other decision makers.
2) He was emotionally challenged to honour family.
3) They followed a roundabout route.
4) His army ran out of water because of the route they took. They nearly died.

When it comes to business success or recovery, a king-in-business cannot afford to make emotional decisions, putting his purpose on the line just to keep up an appearance before his extended family or long standing friends. Making decisions when you are unequally yoked often results in you having to accept the majority or popular vote—rather than the Godly one. This is exactly how Jehoshaphat found himself in the predicament where they ran out of water through taking a roundabout way. They were very close to being overcome by their circumstances, but because he was only a voice amongst others, the leading of God was not considered until it was almost too late. A business king must be able to call upon God and hear from Him to avoid landing in pressurized situations that can cause much damage.

One of the positives that this passage presents is the fact that even though Jehoshaphat had aligned himself with those who didn't know God, when he asked for help from the prophet, it was granted but only because 'he' was amongst the party seeking help. Righteousness was present amidst unrighteousness and God heard the righteous cry. When making decisions as a business king for God, it is crucial to have the leading of God firstly, and not just opinions from those deemed to be wise in the marketplace. They would operate on their skill and knowledge, whereas God knows the beginning from the end. It was very wise of Jehoshaphat to seek and ask if a prophet of God was in the vicinity. Without his input, all would have been lost. Prophetic insight, especially if it is from a proven, reliable source, should be part of a business king's amour.

> But Jehoshaphat said,
> "Is there no prophet of the Lord here,
> that we may inquire of the Lord by him?"
> So one of the servants of the king of Israel
> answered and said,
> "Elisha the son of Shaphat is here, who
> poured water on the hands of Elijah."
> And Jehoshaphat said, "The word of
> the Lord is with him." So the king of
> Israel and Jehoshaphat and the king of
> Edom went down to him.
> Then Elisha said to the king of
> Israel, "What have I to do with you? Go
> to the prophets of your father and the
> prophets of your mother."
> But the king of Israel said to him, "No,
> for the Lord has called these three
> kings together to deliver them into the
> hand of Moab."
>
> (2 Kings 3:11-13)

Be careful with whom you align yourself, and which voice leads you into battle!

DIG CATCHMENT AREAS FIRST

In **2 Kings 3:16**-17, as Elisha waited on God, the Spirit of the Lord told him to tell Jehoshaphat to dig holes and make the valley they were in full of ditches. Elisha told them God would fill the ditches with water for them but they would not see rain, nor hear the wind, nor know how the ditches became full. God would do it. This would be a supernatural provision for them.

It is also good advice for practicing kings-in-business. They are normally used to setting plans in motion to achieve desired results and then monitoring exactly how things are progressing. This is good business practice and should be continued; but a financial king should also remember that God is the source of his business and He provides sometimes in ways that cannot be monitored. You may have an idea of how things will result, but God has so many other sources that you are not even aware of. He can fill your barns with harvest and supply and it doesn't have to come to you in the conventional or expected way. This is what is so exciting about being in relationship with God as a business king. You can do what you know and it will be good. But God can add what you don't know and it will be very good.

The word came from the Lord, **"…Make this valley full of ditches." (v16)** When business is slow or encountering pressure from collapsed markets and economic recessions, God's principles still work. They are not under duress. They have stood the test of time and every attack imaginable. They work despite the circumstances and the answer to Jehoshaphat's situation was in line with how business kings should think about their businesses, particularly their finances. You have to dig holes before God can fill them! Water has to be **captured** and unless you have created **catchment areas**, you will not succeed. There is no harvest unless you first have seed in the ground. To reap you must first sow. Jehoshaphat was told that to capture the water that would save them and their livestock, they would have to dig ditches in faith giving God something to fill. Notice also that God said to dig the valley *full* of ditches. God was not providing for them to just survive. He wanted them to have more than enough because there was also a return journey.

Whenever your business needs cash flow or new business, it is imperative to follow this principle of creating room for God to fill your barns. First, sow generously (dig ditches) and then watch how amazingly God brings returns from unexpected sources. Perhaps you could find other Christian businesses that are struggling and in need of help and donate to them, making it possible for them to turn things around. **(Prov 11:25)** This is how you dig ditches that God will fill in return. God will always provide when His kings make room for Him to supply.

GOD'S TWO-EDGED SWORD

This story also shows us a picture of God's two-edged sword, where He uses both sides to fulfill His purposes. On the one hand, He saved Jehoshaphat and those with him by providing the water they needed; but on the other hand, God allowed what He did for Jehoshaphat to destroy the enemy that had risen up against them. This is the side that kings-in-business don't always expect. I find this amazing about God's two-edged sword. He never just does one thing. When God shows His hand, it not only secures you a future and a hope, but it also destroys the work and advances of the enemy sent to oppose you. The same passage through the Red Sea that saved Israel from the pursuing Egyptians was the same pathway God used to destroy Pharaoh's chariots as they pursued Israel. God used the same water that saved Jehoshaphat and their livestock to also destroy the armies from Moab who had drawn up to oppose them.

**Then they rose up early in the morning,
and the sun was shining on the water; and
the Moabites saw the water on the other
side as red as blood. And they said, "This
is blood; the kings have surely struck
swords and have killed one another; now
therefore, Moab, to the spoil!"
So when they came to the camp of Israel,
Israel rose up and attacked the Moabites,
so that they fled before them; and they
entered their land, killing the Moabites.**

(2 Kings 3:22-24)

God used the water to confuse the Moabites. It was their
land, and they knew it had no water reserves. The sun
created the look of blood in the valley, which lowered their
defenses—they assumed that Israel had turned on each
other, so they moved toward Israel for the kill.

When God suggests that His business kings dig ditches in
their valley experiences, He knows what He is capable of
doing. He knows the results He wants to create. His plan
leads to a full result. As you obey, you are in for a two-
edged sword blessing. Don't hesitate. God is watching over
His word to perform it. The enemy won't be expecting
what will come his way!

Chapter Ten

SPEAKING CREATIVELY

"You will also declare a thing,
And it will be established for you;
So light will shine on your ways."

(Job 22:28)

You visit the earth and water it,
You greatly enrich it;
The river of God is full of water;
You provide their grain,
For so You have prepared it.
You water its ridges abundantly,
You settle its furrows;
You make it soft with showers,
You bless its growth.
You crown the year with Your goodness,
And Your paths drip with abundance.
They drop on the pastures of the
wilderness,
And the little hills rejoice on every side.

(Psalm 65:9-12)

POWER IN DECLARATION

Kings-in-business won't see changes in their circumstances until they can change their own expectations of what they believe God can and will do. Doing more of the same produces what you have been receiving already. What you initiate creates the opportunity for change, because then you have established a drive that you want to see implemented. Speaking and declaring what you are aiming for creates the platform for God to work and unlock the miraculous. Faith frames your future and it is the most crucial ingredient to calling the unseen into a now reality. Faith is the only ingredient that pleases God. Without it, the Bible says, **"…it is impossible to please Him…" (Heb 11:6)** Don't be afraid to copy God. He **"…gives life to the dead and calls those things which do not exist as though they did." (Rom 4:17)** Call those things that aren't, as if they are!

You **frame** your world by the **faith** that you declare and by the **expectations** that you are aiming at. If I am not expecting things to change, recover, or increase in a particular way, then I am just bobbing along in a coasting mode, and hoping something different will emerge. Nothing really changes until you do. Nothing can shift until you create an expectancy of a shift. A king-in-business would be foolish not to establish his goals and desires by what he declares. In so doing he keeps his goals current, focused, and expectant. He stays in a "Faith Zone."

If you aim at nothing, you will hit it. That's no maybe. That's a definite. The world came about because God had an expectation of what He wanted and then declared certain things into existence. We live today in what God spoke and declared as an expectation. He called what wasn't into existence.

Business kings must get used to declaring the success of their businesses and increase to their sales as a normal practice. Their land is a good land and as our opening scripture indicates, God will **"…visit it and water it." (Psalm 65:9)** God wants it to succeed. They should be speaking about its life and progress even in the hardest seasons. They must remain expectant. They should see its success with the eye of faith and speak about its recovery even before it has become a reality. The prophet Isaiah shows more of this concept:

> **"Sing, O barren,**
> **You who have not borne!**
> **Break forth into singing, and cry aloud,**
> **You who have not labored with child!**
> **For more are the children of the desolate**
> **Than the children of the married**
> **woman," says the Lord.**
>
> **(Isaiah 54:1)**

How does the barren woman end up with more than the married one? She was singing her expectancy and making her faith declarations in the same spirit of faith that God called a non-existent world into existence.

This may feel strange and awkward to begin with but it was a dynamic that Jesus also practiced. In **Mark 11**, Jesus spoke to a fig tree, and very shortly after He had, it withered up from the roots. Whatever He said or declared over it was obviously pointed. This is what He was referring to when He said, **"Have faith in God." (v22)** What you speak to the mountains in your way will occur when there is an active expectation. Jesus was teaching us the power there is in speaking, releasing, and declaring things in faith. This should become a part of the business king's behaviour. He should become familiar with the process of creating what he believes through his faith declarations and expectations. He must get used to framing the progress and growth of his business by what he speaks and releases with expectation.

THE POWER OF FAITH EXPECTANCY

Faith expectancy affects several crucial areas of our lives:

1. **Faith expectancy challenges the way we speak.**

Businesses face strong challenges that seem to be able to arrive from almost anywhere. When this happens often enough, the business king could be tempted to think and expect the worst. A lot of the same can condition you to keep expecting more of the same. That is why a lifestyle of faith and creative expectancy is important. When you can change the way you speak and what you expect, that is when Jesus can work and change things to what they need to be.

Jesus often made mention of this principle when He saw people operating in it. This was practice that obviously pleased God. He would say things like, **"...Your faith has made you well," (Luke 17:19)** or **"...According to your faith let it be to you." (Matthew 9:29)** Most outcomes in business are determined by hard work, skill in the marketplace, and a faith expectancy and belief of what your business can do.

We learn from the spies in **Numbers 13** just how devastating a negative mindset can be:

> **"There we saw the giants (the descendants of Anak came from the giants); and we were like grasshoppers in our own sight, and so we were in their sight."**
>
> **(Numbers 13:33)**

This shows that the way you perceive yourself is exactly the way your enemy or your opposition will see you. You need to be able to stand up on the inside for him to realize he has a battle on his hands and you are not just going to go away. If you show yourself to have a focused expectation that your business is positive and successful, then that is how you are perceived. This is the kind of business king that makes the devil have serious concerns. He realizes that you know your end result and nothing will deter you from what you are expecting. When the negative comes, he knows you have an understanding to change the way things are perceived to what they need to become. In the middle of **Job's** worst hardship, when his wife was telling him it would be better to curse God and die; where he had lost his children, home, wealth, financial stability; and where his best friends were telling him that the extent of his suffering was as a result of being an awfully bad sinner; Job changed the outcome. He set in motion the creative expectation that would eventually turn things around and pay him back double for his losses. In that terrible place of suffering and uncertainty he declared, **"You have granted me life and favour, And Your care has preserved my spirit." (Job 10:12)**

Here was a man holding on to what he knew about God. What he was going through was not the final picture. He knew that this time would pass and that God's pres-ervation would present itself. **(Job 42:8-12)** Being able to release an expectation of creative faith, despite your circumstances, is the catalyst that opposes the attack you are enduring and is able to produce a good result.

2.   Faith expectancy affects what happens in your world.

Jesus teaches that God is able to do in your circumstances what you believe and expect He can do.

Business kings must create this expectancy daily. When you do, God can move supernaturally. God is never short on knowing what to do, or how to help people, but He does allow you the opportunity to create the atmosphere for His miraculous. He chooses to work with you. As a result, we need to make a shift in what we are expecting from Him, if we are to see the changes we require. Establish the right atmosphere for God to show Himself faithful. Note what Jesus taught in this regard:

> **But Jesus said to them, "A prophet is not without honour except in his own country, among his own relatives, and in his own house." Now He could do no mighty work there, except that He laid His hands on a few sick people and healed them. And He marveled because of their unbelief. Then He went about the villages in a circuit, teaching.**
>
> **(Mark 6:4-6)**

These people were obviously familiar with Jesus. They knew Him as one who had grown up in their area. Although He was honoured elsewhere in His gifting, at home he wasn't. Isn't this Joseph's son, the carpenter who lived down the road? The result was that because they knew Him, there was no expectancy of what could be done. Your faith and expectations are keys to your outcomes. Familiarity is deadly. You must know who it was that called you to be a **business king** and keep that relationship alive, in faith, and to the highest degree of honour. Then the miraculous has every chance of appearing.

The story of Bartimaeus in **Mark 10** adds support to these thoughts. Even though he was a blind beggar that everyone bore witness to, Jesus still asked him, **"What do you want Me to do for you?"** (Mark 10:51) Someone wearing a beggar's garment and carrying a stick as blind people do, creates an obvious picture of their need. So why ask what he wanted done for himself? You need to be clear on what it is you are expecting from God. You need to state it clearly. Too many times business kings go on their way in their daily routines not really focused on what they expect. When Bartimaeus revealed what he wanted, Jesus replied, **"Go your way; your faith has made you well."** (v52)

The business king encourages a platform for recovery and God's miracles when there is a solid balance between:

    a. A hard and diligent work ethic.
    b. Integrity of business operations.
    c. The use of their skill in the marketplace.
    d. A determined faith expectation.

3. Faith expectation removes barriers that create boxes.

Noah had never seen rain before. He did not know what it was. Yet when divinely warned of unseen dangers, he moved with Godly fear and prepared an ark for the safety of his household. This act of faith obedience framed the future for him. 120 years later (the time it took to complete the task), his household was saved by the substance of that faith. When the flood arrived that would destroy the world **(Heb 11:7)** he had created what would preserve his family.

Your future and recovery in business depends largely on what you see, expect, and release **now** in your current situations. If the fruit you currently produce is not what you want, then shift and adjust things now, so that your future results are closer to what you envisage. Remember that faith is **NOW**. Formulate your future by the expectations you are declaring today. Don't stay in a box that produces more of the same. You must act.

There are numerous examples in the Word of God, where God shows He is definitely interested in restoration and recovery, even if things appear to have very little chance of a now change. When he was sold into slavery by his own brothers, did **Joseph** ever think he would see his family again? Yet God brought a change in global economics (a severe famine) and used Joseph to inspire a world recovery that put him in touch with his long-lost family. Did **Israel** ever think they would not be slaves in Egypt? After 400-plus years as slaves they were conditioned to accept their lot in life. They probably never thought they would get to leave Egypt free, wealthy, and in charge of their own destiny. God shows us over and over again that He is more than able to bring change in our circumstances by creating shifts in what has prevailed for long periods of time. He can do the same with your business. That is why expectation and faith go a long way toward framing the future you desire.

A MEDITATION

This is a word that business and marketplace kings can use as a foundation for their own declarations of faith expectancy:

> **You visit the earth and water it,**
> **You greatly enrich it;**

The river of God is full of water;
You provide their grain,
For so You have prepared it.
You water its ridges abundantly,
You settle its furrows;
You make it soft with showers,
You bless its growth.
You crown the year with Your goodness,
And Your paths drip with abundance.
They drop on the pastures of the
wilderness,
And the little hills rejoice on every side.
The pastures are clothed with flocks;
The valleys also are covered with grain;
They shout for joy, they also sing.

(Psalm 65:9-13)

At the end of each financial year, business kings would do well to spend time alone with God. Go away and worship God and celebrate communion with Him. Remind yourself again who your resource is and that He will be faithful in the coming year. Take the cheque you are about to lay at the apostle's feet. This is a **tithe** of the **spoil** from your previous year's business conquests. Praise God for it and willingly give it into your storehouse with grateful thanks. God has kept you through the word of His Priest and provided for you throughout the seasons of trade this past year. The cheque in your hand is the proof of His goodness. It also serves as the **seed** for the coming year. Honour Him for His goodness and faithfulness. This is all done in the secret place where you personally thank God for what He has done for your business.

The **first** level of the business king's faith expectation according to **Psalm 65** should be a declaration of success and a crowning of the year with the goodness of God. So as you thank God for the previous year's successes, you are coming before Him in faith expectation and declaring the coming year's outcomes as well. You begin the new financial year by releasing the EXPECTATIONS of **Psalm 65:9-13** in faith. We are the seed of Abraham and by faith walk before God under a covenant of blessing. You will succeed and prosper as a business king ought, if you operate correctly and in the spirit of faith.

You declare according to the Psalm:

1) My pastures will always be covered with grain. (The places where business is expected to be conducted will be able to feed and bless my business.) **(v13)**
2) My paths will drip with abundance and teem with flocks. (Leads and opportunities will result in effective harvests.) **(v11)**
3) My year will be crowned with the goodness of God. (The crowning glory at year's end will be the evidence of God's goodness overall. Even as I may endure tough economic times and unsteady trade because of the state of the markets, my expectation of seeing HIS goodness in my business remains.) **(v11)**
4) God, Your goodness is my portion. (The word *goodness* implies things that are most pleasant, prosperous, and dripping with the **welfare** of God. It also carries with it an understanding that God is prepared to change what is current in my circumstances to the way things need to be in reality.)

Business kings should set and state their expectations annually before God. The sowing of the previous year's spoil is vitally important. It is an acknowledgement of thanks and an act of expectant faith. Then once you have

dug the holes to capture the **rain** in your valley of operation (established by your actions of generous giving, sowing of your seed, and your expectant faith declarations), God now has something to fill throughout the year. You have made room to receive what is not yet a reality. Without knowing how, God will see to it. **(2 Kings 3:16)** The giving of your tithe (a seed of all your increase) keeps the door open for God to bless your business with a good harvest. No matter what transpires during the course of the financial year, your focus is on the end result where God has promised to **crown your year with goodness.** You have worked with His principles (faith, expectations, anointing in your skill and giving) and have now positioned yourself for another great year. You may lose some battles during the course of the year but this meditation **(Psalm 65)** will help raise your focus on God's promised end result. A **second** level of faith declaration can also be considered when the season is hard and business tough.

We can believe that God will:

1) **Visit (v9)** our business. The word "visit" here means, *to give attention to.* During your financial trade year, you trust and declare that God will give your business attention, with the express purpose of helping and providing what it will need to succeed. There are always good and indifferent times in business. Sometimes it appears that things are racing ahead, while at other times, things can slow down quite considerably. But your promise is secure. God has provided the "grain" and will provide the necessary "water" to "enrich" it because **His river is full of water.** What you can't see— the unknown of exactly how your provision will come—is not to be

a concern for us. It's God's business; it is His river of supply. He knows what grain you need when.

2) Address the **ridges** and **furrows. (v10)** This language suggests that there will be evidence of hard and tough times that may make things a little bumpy. When business is slow it creates pressure on cash flow and causes problems for your creditors. However this Psalm promises that God will send **"rain"** and **"soft showers"** to **"settle the furrows"** so that growth will be maintained. God will bless the business with a fruitful return by sending unexpected blessings in those tough economic times—enough to settle your ridges and furrows—so that you will still see a profit.

The king-in-business would be wise to set aside time with God at the beginning of each financial year and meditate on this Psalm. They can bring before God their targets, goals, and expectations of faith for the business. They are also able to stand in faith throughout the year by believing God to crown their year with success and evidence of His goodness. God's visiting (giving the business attention) regardless of the economic season, will accomplish this. Every ridge and furrow will be subject to the soft showers of His provision undergirding all that they require to profit, even in the least expectant times. When others know that winter is coming and a time of leanness is about to arrive, God's business kings have confidence that God will ensure a maintained provision.

What hope we have as HIS business kings!

Chapter Eleven

SWIMMING UPSTREAM

**And the sons of the prophets said to
Elisha, "See now, the place where we
dwell with you is too small for us. Please,
let us go to the Jordan, and let every man
take a beam from there, and let us make
there a place where we may dwell."
So he answered, "Go."
Then one said, "Please consent to go with
your servants."
And he answered, "I will go."** So he went
**with them. And when they came to the
Jordan, they cut down trees. But as one
was cutting down a tree, the
iron ax head fell into the water; and he
cried out and said, "Alas, master! For it
was borrowed."
So the man of God said, "Where did it
fall?"** And he showed him the place. **So he
cut off a stick, and threw it in there; and
he made the iron float. Therefore he said,
"Pick it up for yourself."** So he reached
out his hand and took it.

(2 Kings 6:1-7)

BUSINESS KINGS DRIVE THEMSELVES ONWARDS

One of the most amazing phenomena in nature has to be the
annual migration of salmon back to their spawning

grounds. No matter where these grounds are they make their way back and re-enter the rivers that began their journey in life. Once they reach these rivers, the whole experience becomes a battle and determination to swim upstream until they reach their destination. There they spawn and millions of new eggs become fertilized to ensure that the salmon cycle lives on. How these fish negotiate the hazards of this experience is simply amazing. They literally swim against the flow of the river, jump up over waterfalls and rapids, negotiate weirs, and swim the gauntlet past thousands of hungry bears waiting to plunder their numbers for much-needed protein and storage fat for the winter. It seems that the drive within is so strong that it catapults them onwards and upwards against all odds until they finally reach their breeding grounds. These fish show that they are extremely **task orientated** and **determined to succeed.** Obstacles are an expected experience and not a signal that it is too tough to go on and that it would much easier to turn with the flow than swim against it.

Business and marketplace kings must accept that they function in one of the toughest arenas known to man. Being a business king is not for the faint-hearted. To succeed in this arena they must possess a drive to keep them moving towards the goals they need to accomplish. Even when it feels to them that they are the only ones having to swim upstream, they have to have the ability to push against the flow. They have to be able to defy gravity and the natural pull of the world markets if they are moving in an opposite direction. For example, when markets collapse and banks stop lending; and when petrol prices, interest rates, and credit restraints soar; these all band together to cause a downward spiral that results in very little activity in the marketplace. People become afraid to trade because of the uncertain markets and this has a devastating effect down the line on homeowners and small businesses. People struggle to pay bills and banks start to call in their bonds and mortgages and panic arrives in no uncertain terms. Big companies and small business owners start talking about downsizing, layoffs, and shorter working hours because they no longer have the means to keep going as they had been in happier economic climates.

This action in the marketplace forces a strong downstream spiral. The collapses in the economy cause this natural downward flow and it gathers a momentum that proves very hard to resist. When everyone is going in one direction and you need to swim upstream, you will have to have some drive, some motivation, something that allows you to defy gravity and push against the flow at all costs.

This is where the salmon are a good example for us to follow. You CAN swim upstream. You can defy the world trends because you are not on the world's economy markets. You are on God's economic plan. His plan hasn't failed, nor is it ever going to fail. Business kings must possess the call of financial kingship and trust in the anointing with which God has equipped them. You are primed to succeed despite the economic climate. If God can cause Isaac to sow in a famine and reap a hundred fold in the same year, He can help you go against the flow and succeed where people and institutions least expect it. **(Gen 26:1-3; 12-16)** Often (make sure it is so in your case) when the world is telling you to slow down, sell off, and downsize, it could be God's opportunity for you to seize the moment and **"Enlarge the place of your tent And let them stretch out the curtains of your dwellings; Do not spare; Lengthen your cords, And strengthen your stakes." (Isa 54:2)** God has a way to cause His business kings to prosper and be able to swim upstream when everyone else is panicking.

As business kings you will be affected by the changes and challenges to the economy and markets. You will feel the pressure they produce, but the one trump card you have is that God's economy isn't controlled by what happens here on earth. If you are doing what God has asked you to do and you have been obeying God's economic principles that govern the financial arena, God will see to it that you prosper and succeed. You will succeed in swimming upstream no matter how strong the flow in the opposite direction. You will make it to God's planned purpose for you. Keep your faith and trust strong and your eyes on God and pray for a sensitivity to know what God is saying to you. Use the skill He has given you to operate in the marketplace and He will show you how to negotiate the obstacles that suddenly appear. If salmon can do it, how much more able are the anointed financial kings that God has set apart in this function?

PRINCIPLES TO HELP DEFY GRAVITY (from 2 Kings 6)

1. **Expanding God's purpose for your business (v1)**

Expansion and growth are all good desires and signs of solid leadership and great decisions made at the right times. However, the business king needs to guard against **greed.** It has a way of causing you to chase things that supposedly lead to more money, but can prove to be disastrous. Remember your business is God's. He is the CEO and unless it is God connecting and colliding you with new opportunities, don't fall into the trap of chasing easy money.

The sons of the prophet spoke to Elisha saying, "**'See now, the place where we dwell with you is too small for us.'**" **(v1)** If God is directing you to expand He will see to it that regardless of the market performances, you will maintain and increase in all economic climates.

When God is the initiator of your growth, you will always be able to swim upstream where others succumb to the force of gravity. What God initiates always has the ability to self-perpetuate. The story of creation in **Genesis 1** confirms this. God made sure that there was seed within the seed so that what was created once could be re-created again and again. **(Gen 1:11-12)** You will always defy the natural pull of market-related gravity and be able to expand—as long as God is the initiator.

2. **Knowing that I'm part of God's planned answer (v2)**

Ephesians 4:16 tells us that the body of Christ will grow and develop when each part is doing what it is supposed to do. This is one of the major growth and expansion principles contained in the word of God. In our story we read, **"'...and let every man take a beam from there, and let us make there a place where we may dwell.'" (v2)** The house is built when each part does its part. This is the secret to biblical growth.

Business kings are chosen and appointed by God and placed strategically in local churches. Each church needs to recognise and develop this financial king section. They are a provisionary answer from God. Their anointing has the ability to advance the kingdom of God and fund the purpose of the local church. When each financial king **brings his beam** (his financial support) to where God has planted him, their local church will become an effective blessing in the community and will be able to accomplish God's purpose for it. Kings need to realize that they are part of God's handpicked strategy to create increase and growth where they fellowship. As they play their part in His strategy, God will always help them find a way to swim upstream and preserve them safely in the tough economic climates and unexpected changes that frequent the marketplace.

3. Attaining permission from God (v2)

Being able to hear the rhema words of God is crucial for your success when you encounter waterfalls, pitfalls, and economic obstacles sent to throw you off course. When the storm raged at sea, Peter didn't just get out of the boat and walk on the water to Jesus. He first asked permission from the Lord, and only then did he act on what Jesus said.

God's rhema words are **now** words in your current circumstances. They are what make the difference between success and failure. Obedience to them will always result in success because they are God's 'now' answers for you and are backed by the scripture when Jesus said, **"'...and the gates of Hades shall not prevail against it.'" (Matt 16:18)** Alighting on a project that God has not authenticated will result in the waves of the storm engulfing you; but moving out with His permission will ensure that you swim upstream against the flow of everything going the opposite way. It is absolutely imperative to hear God's **now** word to your situation. This is where you have the confidence to expect what God has said.

4. The presence of your man of God (v3)

A significant misunderstanding in the church today is the role and authority of the man God has placed over you. Submission to this spiritual authority is a key ingredient to your financial success and the release of the harvest designated by God for your destiny. The position he occupies in your life contributes greatly to the success you will enjoy in your business. Honouring this gift by following the leading of the Spirit through his preaching and counsel, paves the way for God to release blessing to you.

When Moses assembled the first priesthood in the wilderness after Israel left Egypt, Aaron was instructed by Moses, after hearing God on the subject, to **bless** the people of God. There was a particular way God wanted it done. Part of the priest's function in the New Testament is releasing the power of **blessing** over his people and their circumstances. They are required to unlock the promises of God to their congregations and afford them the opportunity of experiencing the power to succeed. This was to be pronounced over them in the form of a spoken blessing. Your man of God should be speaking prophetically to you and praying the release of the **blessings of God** for your business. **(Num 6:22-27)** He has been anointed to **bless** you and keep your operational borders expanding. He is a vital figure to the business king's progress in the marketplace.

5. Place value on my ax head (v5)

The tools these servants had to build a larger meeting place included discernment, passion, a word of approval from the prophet of God, and an **iron ax head.** This ax head was the cutting tool to bring the resources that were required to complete the task. Without the ax head in use, there was no possibility of collecting the resources. This ax head had to be sharp and ready to be put into effective usage. Keeping it that way and operational was a necessity.

So when one of the servants lost his ax head in the river he was distraught and cried out to Elisha for help. He understood that without this tool to retrieve the resources, he was not an active part of the plan to expand their vision.

God's financial kings need to realize what they have been given by God. Your businesses are the ax heads that lead to resources being gathered, so that the church will be in a good position to win the lost and advance the kingdom. Your ax head must be a producer and a supplier that can assist the purpose God has for you. You should value not only your ax head (business) but also the opportunity to be part of God's financial resource team. To understand that God has selected and placed an anointing on you to gather in and transfer your portion of the marketplace spoil into the hands of the priests and prophetic figures who have kingdom vision, is a must for all potential kings-in-business. Kings who understand this would be just as distraught as the servant in our story, should they realize that they have lost the effective purpose of their ax head. These kings understand that it is not about chasing money, but their successful function in the marketplace provides the ability for the church to reach the lost more effectively and advance the kingdom of God rapidly. This is the whole point of kings becoming wealthy conduits of finance in the kingdom. Thankfully there is a way to recover if your ax head is lost or has become dulled and unproductive.

6. Retrace your steps to where your ax head fell (v6)

An amazing phenomenon when following God is that when you derail your purpose for whatever reasons, God always has a plan to restore to you what has been lost. He always seems to have a way that we have not thought about or considered. In many cases God will take us back to where we lost sight of the original purpose. The first question Elisha asked was, **"Where**

did it fall?" (v6) and because the servant could show him the place, Elisha was able to assist and give prophetic instruction that would lead to the ax head's recovery. Never discount the prophetic word that God releases. You prosper when you obey an accurate prophetic word. It was through the prophet's word that the ax head was restored to the servant.

As long as you follow the guidelines that the New Testament records for the prophetic, you will have at your disposal a powerful tool that will prove invaluable to your business kingship.

As a king-in-business it is possible to lose focus and take wrong turns that lead away from the original plan of God for your success. As soon as you feel that your ax head is blunt or no longer effective, trace back to where it was derailed and find the mistake or wrong turn you made. Apply the adjustments necessary to get yourself back on track and in due season you will find yourself recovering well. Suddenly you will notice that the ax head has been sharpened again and production is picking up. God has caused it to miraculously float up against gravity, and against all odds find that it is productive again. Everything that contributed to it sinking to the riverbed below is now null and void.

7. Apply the power of the cross (v6)

There are a few stories in the Bible where the power of the cross is symbolized by a stick being placed directly into a particular circumstance with amazing results.

One example is at the waters of **Marah** where Israel came to drink during their wilderness journey with Moses. When they arrived, they found the water so bitter that it was unpalatable. **(Exod 15:23-25)** Whilst the people voiced their disapproval and murmured against Moses, God told Moses to cut a stick from a nearby bush and throw it into the water. As the stick touched the water, it changed and became drinkable. The fruit of the cross experience always turns bitter experiences into sweet ones.

Another time when a stick was used is in our story with the ax head. Elisha also threw a stick into the water where the ax head was lost and the iron ax head floated up to the stick—against the natural pull of gravity. Recovery is often a swim upstream. Don't give up before you even start.

Kings-in-business should never underestimate the power of the cross when considering their businesses. The story of the cross has so many amazing angles to it. It speaks of the goodness of God, His mercy and kindness for a sinful world where Jesus, our spotless lamb, was sacrificed so that heaven and eternal life could be opened up for all. Paul talks about it being **"...the power of God to salvation..." (Rom 1:16)** The cross was where the enemy (the devil) was finally defeated. The power of darkness was destroyed on the cross at Calvary and all who believe and trust in this supreme, voluntary sacrifice, and accept Jesus as the one sent by God to die for us and cleanse us from our sins, can walk in the power of all it represented.

> **"And as Moses lifted up the serpent in the wilderness, even so must the Son of Man be lifted up, that whoever believes in Him should not perish but have eternal life."**
>
> **(John 3:14-15)**

The cross has supernatural power attached to its significance. Moses made a bronze snake in the desert and put it on a pole and all who had been bitten by snakes in the wilderness lived, when they looked at this bronze snake. **(Num 21:9)** Those who have been bitten by the world and lost in sin, or bitten by circumstances where everything appears lifeless, need to do what Elisha did in our story. He threw in a stick—symbolic of the cross—where the ax head was lost and it floated up to the stick on the surface. The bitter experience became sweet. The ax head defied the laws of gravity and **swam upstream** against all odds. This is what the power of the cross and Jesus' sacrifice on it can mean for your business as well. God can make it swim upstream amidst the toughest economic conditions.

As you repent of where you made wrong turns away from God's plans for you, you place yourself in the position where God can resurrect what should be and you create the distinct possibility of having things turned around for you. Repent if you have moved away from what God gave you. Speak and declare the prophetic word where you lost the plot. Believe again what God has said previously and act accordingly. **Matthew 19:26** reminds us that, **"...with God all things are possible."** If God can cause an iron ax head to float upstream, He can do something supernatural in your business.

8. Keep going when there are setbacks (v7)

After Elisha had thrown in the stick where the ax head had been lost and the ax head floated to the surface, he turned to the one who had lost it and said, **"Pick it up for yourself." (v7)**

Often when you just start out in business or you begin a project, you experience an unexpected attack designed to stop your progress. The last thing our enemy wants from the business king is success in his purpose. The best time to derail your purpose in the projects you are undertaking is in the beginning stages. This is the time when tensions are high and expectations are great. A good beginning is a real positive, but also a successful attack becomes a real vision destroyer. You can trace back and see how often an attack came in the Word of God, when a project was still in its infancy stages. In the lives of **Moses** and **Jesus** alone, whilst they were still tiny infants, a call went out to kill them. Moses survived by being hidden in the bushes and Jesus was taken to Egypt for a while, after an angel had a word with his parents.

The servant in our story had only just begun to cut timber for the enlargement project when the ax head disappeared in the river. Sometimes it's hard to continue when you suffer setbacks and losses as you implement the dreams you believe are from God. In hindsight though, these setbacks can become the building blocks of your future. Most times the things that happen to you are sent as distractions from the real purpose. I am sure that Joseph (Jacob's son) was able to keep going through all the things he endured (13 years of servitude) because they were not in the dreams he had originally seen. You have a dream, a project, a purpose to fulfill. The ax head loss was not part of the original planning, so don't allow these setbacks to become the main play of your focus. Keep your vision on what God has shown you, because that is what will eventually materialize.

The message here is clear. Don't give up on your purpose. YOU have to **pick up your ax head** and keep going. God gave the dream to you. You need to run with it. If you lost your ax head, 'you' need to pursue after it and find it again so that you can continue. Even though you may receive help along the way, you will still need to retrieve your ax head for yourself. Only you can fulfill what it is that God has given you to do. You must show the confidence to do so. God has believed in you. Believe now in what He sees you can do. Don't sit back and wait for him to carry on for you. He needs you to recover and find your cutting-edge again.

Chapter Twelve

INTENSITY CREATES MOMENTUM TO RECEIVE

Then he said, "Take the arrows"; so he took them. And he said to the king of Israel, "Strike the ground"; so he struck three times, and stopped. And the man of God was angry with him, and said, "You should have struck five or six times; then you would have struck Syria till you had destroyed it! But now you will strike Syria only three times."

(2 Kings 13:18-19)

**Do not eat the bread of a miser,
Nor desire his delicacies;
For as he thinks in his heart, so is he.**

(Proverbs 23:6-7)

AS A BUSINESS KING THINKS, SO IS HE

Proverbs 23:7 reminds us that what a person thinks in his heart is very important to the outcome. How you think about your business will affect how you behave, and this is a crucial recovery step when you need to move things from where they are currently, to where they need to be. The business king, like many others, is subject to various attacks in the marketplace designed to hinder, distract, frustrate, and even create doubt in what they are attempting to accomplish. A sustained period of lack is very serious and goes a long way to disturb your peace of mind and unsettle positive decision-making. Hence more reasons for the business kings to be purpose-driven and focused on how they think and approach difficulties. Failure to do this purposefully and strategically could result in disaster.

The recent worldwide economic recession of 2008 that lasted a number of years was devastating, to say the least. Many countries were affected and it resulted, across financial institutions, in all forms of panic, anxiety, and contingency planning having to be put in place. The recession exposed the fragility of many economies and where people thought things were relatively safe, learned that they weren't. Nothing was then or is now guaranteed. Suddenly economies were inundated with desperate thinking plans and the need to cut back, downsize, retrench staff, withhold credit, call money in and do whatever is required to keep costs to a minimum. Millions were seriously affected by this dramatic approach to curb the over-spending that had been allowed and many lost businesses, homes and their security because credit had been withdrawn. Bankruptcy was a common result and many lives and businesses lay in ruins. This wasn't the first economic recession to wreak havoc in the marketplace and it surely will not be the last. We must understand that a world in recession, whilst devastating in one sense, can be an opportunity for others.

> **"I have given them Your word; and the world has hated them because they are not of the world, just as I am not of the world. I do not pray that You should take them out of the world, but that You should keep them from the evil one. They**

are not of the world, just as I am not of the world."

(John 17:14-16)

God's business kings, even though they are subject to the same economic pressures as everyone else, can turn this time into an opportunity. They are in the world but not of it. This is not a cliché. This is a scriptural fact. God's kings-in-business operate in this world but have the advantage of another financial system that can't fail. They operate on God's economic plan and this plan hasn't allowed for world recessions. This plan is not affected or subject to the failures of the world's economy. This plan defies natural logic and produces wealth, cash flow, and increase, despite what is current in the marketplace. It cannot be dictated by what is common in this world. But it will, however, require that your **thinking** be on God's approach to things. You will need to renew your mind and embrace how God thinks and operates in financial terms.

Which farmer would seriously consider sowing in a drought, especially if he knew that the current drought was to be more severe than the memory of a more recent one that was also devastating? Yet in **Genesis 26:1-5**, Isaac heard God tell him to stay where he was and sow in this famine. This defies natural logic but because Isaac was convinced it was God, he obeyed. The obedience led him to a hundred-fold blessing return. To most business kings, a hundred-fold return on your investment would be a great day at the office. But God **"...is able to do exceedingly abundantly above all that we ask or think, according to the power that works in us."** (Eph 3:20)

Notice the word **think.** Isaac had to remove what he thought about the circumstances and what others were saying, and obey what he was hearing from God. It led to this hundred-fold return, which was for a businessman a fantastic achievement, but for God, it was only the starting place of Isaac's blessing.

After the hundred-fold blessing, **Genesis 26:12-13** says, **"...and the Lord blessed him. The man began to prosper, and continued prospering until he became very prosperous."** The key to blessing in a recession and uncertain markets is obedience to God. It makes sure that there is no compliance to the popular panic reactions taking shape in the marketplace. Recessions and economic famines, whilst devastating to say the least, are often the seedbeds to creative, new opportunities. God is never caught short of opening up new and innovative ways to create new business. Business kings just need to keep pressing into God and being expectant of these new opportunities.

When you squeeze a blown-up balloon in your hands, the pressure forces the air in the balloon to find new avenues of escape—suddenly, sections of the balloon form new shapes and sizes in-between the gaps in your fingers. Recession, collapsed markets, and unstable economies are tough and create pressure on what we do in the marketplace. But this same pressure will also establish other forms of escape that were not previously considered, which have now become opportunities.

When Israel was going through a tough time as a nation, the prophet Isaiah wrote:

> **"Enlarge the place of your tent,**
> **And let them stretch out the curtains of**
> **your dwellings;**
> **Do not spare;**
> **Lengthen your cords,**

And strengthen your stakes."

(Isaiah 54:2)

In a place where the economy is tight and things are tough, the normal thinking would be to downsize, close up, and button down the hatches. But this scripture suggests another way to think about pressure. Perhaps business kings should research the new areas of business opportunities that have now surfaced, and instead of a maintenance program, they should think expansion, growth, and a way forward. When Israel arrived at the Red Sea with Pharaoh's army close behind them, God's instruction to Moses was to tell the people to **go forward (Exod 14:15)** even when that seemed impossible. There was no way back from where they were. What better time to show that God's principles work. What a good time to prove the dominion that God's economic strategies actually carry. They work regardless of the state of our economy, but you must hear God first.

Thoughts from our scripture like, **"Do not spare"** or **"Enlarge the place..."** or **"stretch out..."** are not common actions when things get really tough in financial markets. Business kings will have to adjust the way they think because your thoughts often dictate how you will react. Israel lost this battle in **Numbers 13:31** when they decided they were not more than grasshoppers in the eyes of their enemy and conducted themselves in like fashion. God was not pleased and they were turned back into the wilderness to allow time for that generation of hesitant, doubting people, to die out. God wanted a new generation, with a **"different spirit" (Num 14:24)** to enter the Promised Land. To conquer and exercise dominion in the Promised Land would require a different breed of thinkers. This form of intense, creative thinking, can lead to new horizons.

125

Instead of becoming grasshoppers in the face of giants, business kings and those needing to recover should let the enemy see the stature of the giants within themselves. Things turn around when your thinking coincides with God's. Then you act.

BUNDLES OF PURPOSE WAITING IN YOUR PATH

As a business king in the kingdom, there is no substitute for you being purpose-driven and focused. You need to ensure you gain God's **added** package in your personal kingship. **(Matt 6:33)** Setbacks are part of the training ground and those who end up recovering and going on to be great successes are those who pursue their dreams with **passion** and **energy**. They also come to realize that the final goal is the fulfillment of the original dream, but it unravels into its shape, only as they pursue it. Often you only know the starting and end points and have little insight into the stages along the way. Joseph, for example, had great dreams of God's purpose for him but the pit, Potiphar's wife, and prison were not in the initial dream. He had to trust God deeply through these in-between stages.

Ruth discovered this revelation as she gleaned in Boaz's fields. If she hadn't been working through her tough times (her in-between stages), she would not have collided with what God had in mind for her. In **Ruth 2:16**, she didn't realize at first that the bundles of grain that she stumbled across were actually left there **purposefully** for her not to miss. This is just so typical of God's goodness to us. As we love, honour, and obey God in our calling and get on with the daily, often-mundane tasks of running our businesses and lives, God leaves in our paths opportunities for us to bump into. His kings-in-business stumble headfirst into these bundles of blessing and sheer goodness. The **intensity** that Ruth applied to their survival (hers and Naomi's), not only lead to these miracle provisions, but

126

down the road, the same fields she gleaned in as a needy person to keep themselves alive, became hers through her marriage to Boaz. Gleaning in Boaz's fields was also God's purpose for her. She bumped into Boaz, the man God had in mind for her, and the one He would use to fulfill her destiny.

David had a similar experience of bumping into what God purposefully left in his path. His father sent him out one day to find his brothers and bring news of them. They were away at war with King Saul against the Philistine army. He left in **1 Samuel 17:17-18** as a spectator and had no idea that his journey would land him being the main feature on God's agenda. Killing the giant Goliath and meeting King Saul were God's plans to promote and introduce David as a future player in Israel's history. David had no understanding that this battle with Goliath would get him acquainted with the King of Israel and that it was a prophetic picture of his call and destiny. David was on an errand for his father when he collided with this planned purpose from God.

This is the point: that you continue on with **passion** and **intensity** in whatever it is you are doing in your financial kingship and purpose for God. Your recovery is imminent. God is in control. He has arranged **bundles of purpose** for you to collide into so you can connect with your destiny. Keep your expectation, in faith. Stay focused and always expectant that He has 'bundles of goodness' left in your path.

Hagar discovered in **Genesis 16:13-14** that God was all-seeing. When she didn't expect God to be aware of her desperate circumstances, God came to her in the desert and rescued her. She was overwhelmed by **the-God-who-lives-and-sees**-me. This same God is with us today in all our circumstances and in every economic crisis. Your success and growth lies in being able to pursue what you believe

127

God has for you. You will be able to maintain and increase your intensity knowing that the God you can't see, is fully aware of where you are right now in life and He will manifest Himself to you with understanding. The one you don't feel to be with you or near you, is in fact, actively part of your experience. Keep mobile – keep focused – keep moving forward with expectation, because the intensity with which you pursue your dream is often the reason why you achieve it.

STRIKE WITH PASSION

The story of King Joash visiting Elisha before he departed for eternal glory is found in **2 Kings 13:14-19**. It makes fascinating reading and has a great message that points out the valuable roles that **intensity** and **assertion** play in ensuring healthy business returns and recovery. Hard work, diligence, and hearing God are core ingredients to creating success in business.

Syria was, in those days, a thorn to Israel, and the **arrow of deliverance** shot at them from the east window **(v17)** was exactly that. It was aimed at **"Aphek"** (meaning *stronghold*) and was a prophetic picture that this constant thorn in Israel's side was to be destroyed. Elisha placed his hand on the king's hand when he released the arrow, authenticating the power and need for the **prophetic** in a business **king's** life. The shooting of the arrow was to be followed up by the king striking the ground with other arrows. **(v18)** It was this action that would determine the measure of success Israel would eventually have over Syria.

King Joash missed the point completely. Whether he just didn't understand or felt a little embarrassed to strike the arrows on the ground, his actions earned him a sharp rebuke from the prophet. His action showed no conviction, no intensity, and no assertion. He just nonchalantly went through the process as if there was no real purpose to what he was doing. Elisha voiced strong, prophetic views on these actions. **(v19)** King Joash's failure to embrace the moment resulted in little success—certainly not what God had in mind. The Word of God teaches that believing God's prophets results in prosperity. **(2 Chron 20:20)** When you hear the word of God for your situation and receive the guidance of the **prophetic** as King Joash had, that is when you should show your belief and back it up with intensity. Show conviction in your belief that it will be just as God said it would. **(Acts 27: 25)**

This is a trait often absent when trying to recover from financial ruin or other setbacks in life. Your spirit is broken. There is often the sense of hopelessness and it becomes very hard to find the intensity to believe again. But always be encouraged when you hear the prophetic and know that it is God speaking.

> **"God is not a man, that He should lie,**
> **Nor a son of man, that He should repent.**
> **Has He said, and will He not do?**
> **Or has He spoken, and will He not make**
> **it good?"**
>   **(Numbers 23:19)**

You don't want to nullify your faith expectations by a faithless conviction. INTENSIFY – God is with you.

(Please note: For New Testament understanding of the Prophetic, never just do what a Prophetic Ministry says, UNLESS it is a confirmation of what the HOLY SPIRIT has already told you.)

Chapter Thirteen

THE PROPHETIC WORD ABIDES

Then Elisha died, and they buried him. And the raiding bands from Moab invaded the land in the spring of the year. So it was, as they were burying a man, that suddenly they spied a band of raiders; and they put the man in the tomb of Elisha; and when the man was let down and touched the bones of Elisha, he revived and stood on his feet.

(2 Kings 13:20-21)

THE WORD WILL MAKE THINGS GOOD

Some of the strengths that business kings have to hold on to and utilize in combat are their **relationships with God** and their **belief in the power of the Word.** The beauty of knowing what God has said to you means that whatever happens, it will always come about regardless of the time it takes. We seem to feel that if it takes a long time to be fulfilled, then perhaps we got it wrong earlier. God can't lie, nor will He tell you something He didn't mean. Being in a living relationship with God and hearing His rhema words to you, reveals the power there is in the spoken Word of God. God will make good what he has told you. He watches to perform His Word. **(Jer 1:12)**

Apart from Jesus, I know of no man who has walked on water. This is a phenomenon that doesn't ordinarily happen. Why was it possible then for Peter to get out of a boat and walk to Jesus on the rough, turbulent waters of a stormy sea? The answer is simple—Jesus gave him permission. **(Matt 14:29)** He walked on the water because he had the word from God to do so. Knowing God's word to you releases the power to accomplish, in any situation, what God has said. Circumstances don't matter. Also, the power of the word of God won't work if you assume what you want it to do. You must have permission. You must have the Spirit of God speak it to you. You must be in possession of God's **now** word. We live on what proceeds out of the mouth of God. **(Matt 4:4)**

How was it possible for Moses to lift up a rod over the water and divide the Red Sea, providing a pathway for the whole nation of Israel to walk through in complete safety? Imagine a highway through the middle of a deep sea with walls of water as the boundaries. This is not a usual practice in life. What was the reason for this possibility? God gave him the command to do it! God told him to, **"...lift up your rod, and stretch out your hand over the sea and divide it..." (Exod 14:16)**

Once he had the word from God and obeyed the instruction, the Red Sea divided and created a pathway for safe passage. God's word has power and authority to change, create, or alter anything where it has been sent. **(Isa 55:11)**

A business king can trust explicitly the word of the Lord to him in his situation. No matter what the real picture appears to be surrounding his business, the moment he obeys God's spoken word to him, God will make it good. God cannot lie. He is incapable of saying one thing to you, but meaning something else. He always speaks His truth to you. Hearing the now word in your situation is a guarantee that God will confirm what He has said.

DEAD BONES AND THE PROPHETIC

Always keep the promises of God to you alive. In the right time they will reveal the fruit of why they were sent. God promised Jeremiah that He would watch over His word to perform it. **(Jer 1:12)** In short, God will remember what He has sent to you and make sure that it matures at the right time, and under the right circumstances.

Simeon was an old man in the story of **Luke 2:25-27,** but God had promised him that he would not see death until he had seen the consolation of Israel. He had received a **preceding word** that **proceeded** the next phase of his life. Sometime later, Simeon was prompted by the Spirit of God to go to the temple on a certain day and time and his eyes would behold what God had previously promised him. Simeon, which is translated to mean *hear*, lived up to this meaning of his name and got to enjoy the fruit of it. He was able to hear God and it was this hearing ability that kept him alive. He lived in the revelation of what God had ordained to precede his life. Not even death could sneak up on him because the **now** word given earlier had not been fulfilled. Simeon kept the promise of God to him actively focused and alive. The power of it kept him safe and sustained him through life and every circumstance that threatened him. No matter what his life had to endure, whether it was the threat of sickness, financial ruin, or anything else, he was safe because what God has promised him hadn't been fulfilled. Simeon had the backing of a *proceeding word.*

Elisha was an amazing prophet of God and a true gift ministry to Israel. He was anointed prophetically, even to the bone! If you could catch or touch what was on him, you would live. When prophets speak, people in hopeless situations get the opportunity to live, as was told to Abimelech in **Genesis 20:7.** Abimelech was told, **"now therefore restore the man's wife; for he is a prophet, and he will pray for you and YOU SHALL LIVE."** That is the power Prophets carry. The anointing on Elisha was right into his bones, so much so that when a dead person was mistakenly put into his grave and touched them, he came to life immediately. Even if the prophet of God who spoke a word to you is no longer alive, the word spoken to you remains alive until its fulfillment. God tells the prophets what to say. He puts His word in their mouth. **(Jer 1:9)** They live because they are spoken by the inspiration of the Holy Spirit. You need to keep them alive by believing with an expectation what God has revealed.

As kings-in-business we would do well to be around the prophets of God and those who hear what God is saying. Whatever you have been accurately told by His prophets, hold onto those things. They will come to pass, even if they appear to show no life or bearing on where you are at the moment. The bones of the prophet still hold anointing. What may appear to be dead and forgotten, still lives in God. God will not tell you something He didn't intend for you to have. Be careful to observe how to test prophecy as explained in the Word of God. Once you know the word you have received is accurate, you have the proceeding word of God and it will accomplish what it was sent to do.

When I left Bible school I was prayed over and received a word about my future in the ministry. It was way beyond what seemed possible for a young, probationary Pastor from a little insignificant country in Africa. Nothing really happened in conjunction with the word I received (apart from the places of training I would have to endure) for 25 years. This is a long time to wait, but I kept the word alive with expectation. I reminded God of what He had said from time to time and that I was expecting its fulfillment. Then it happened. What God said to me began to unfold and it is still unfolding today. So never give up on what God has spoken. He knows the times and the seasons. He is not a man that He would lie!

"Hear me, O Judah and you inhabitants of Jerusalem: Believe in the Lord your God, and you shall be established; believe His prophets, and you shall prosper."

(2 Chronicles 20:20)

136

Chapter Fourteen

BEHIND CLOSED DOORS

**Then the king of Israel sent someone to
the place of which the man of God had
told him. Thus he warned him, and he
was watchful there, not just once or twice.
Therefore the heart of the king of Syria
was greatly troubled by this thing; and he
called his servants and said to them, "Will
you not show me which of us is for the
king of Israel?"
And one of his servants said, "None, my
lord, O king; but Elisha, the prophet
who is in Israel, tells the king of Israel the
words that you speak in your bedroom."**

(2 Kings 6:10-12)

SECRET LIFE VERSES PUBLIC LIFE

One of the true tests of people and kings-in-business who
profess to follow after the Lord Jesus is the **fruit** that
follows their lives. It's not what you say or do that shows
the real you. You can train yourself to be a public figure
and learn how to conduct yourself appropriately. How
people see you behave in public may not necessarily be a
picture of who you really are.

It is the fruit that you actually produce that measures the
real test of a public life that is trustworthy. Jesus taught us
to look for the fruit. **(Matt 7:15-16)** This is the true test of

any life, purpose, ministry, or organization. The true heart of a business king is measured more accurately by the fruit of his obedience to the call on his life. Is he truly an unselfish provider in the kingdom?

Nothing is hidden for too long. What is practiced and subscribed to in secret will eventually surface. A king-in-business won't be an expressive worshipper in his church life, unless he also worships demonstrably in his secret place. He may do what is required of him financially in the church, but if this action is not a joyous one in private, then he can't be considered to have a generous heart. The giving of your money is a heart issue. Business kings are called to **a ministry of supply**. They need to understand the anointing God has given them and become generous givers so that the kingdom can advance on the earth—so departing with their wealth is a genuine heart issue. A business king doesn't give mechanically, but rather in response to the call of God on his life. The measure of his Kingship Stature is the fruit of his obedient giving in response to the understanding of his purpose from God.

 Jesus taught that if a person was honest and reliable with a little money, then he could be trusted with a lot more money. **(Matt 25)** The fruit that is produced when you handle much comes from the practice you displayed when you handled little. Before you will give generously from your abundance, you need to show that you can give generously from your limited supply.

Joseph showed he was trustworthy and proved to be a faithful prime minister over Egypt by first producing the fruit of reliability with another man's goods and then by the fruit he produced in prison. **(Genesis 39-41)** This was real fruit because there was no one to witness it. What he did outside the view of the public eye was the fruit he produced when he became a public figure. Most often the success you enjoy publically is as a result of what people don't see behind closed doors. You may not feel that people notice things, but they do. You produce fruit regardless of whether it is good or bad. Watch how you live. Strive to be in public what you are in secret. If you don't like your secret life, initiate change quickly, because the fruit of it will be exposed in due season.

WATCH THE WORDS SPOKEN IN SECRET

The King of Syria became frustrated with his war cabinet because he thought he had a spy in his ranks. **(v11)** Everything he planned against Israel, even to the last detail of where they would be and when, somehow was intercepted. It seemed that Israel always had 'wind' of his strategic plans. The explanation was simple enough:

> **And one of his servants said, "None, my lord, O King: but Elisha the prophet who is in Israel, tells the king of Israel the words that you speak in your bedroom."**
> **(2 Kings 6:12)**

What this king spoke in private somehow became public knowledge later. However, this was not because of a spy in his ranks or anything sinister, but simply the result of an anointing of God on a gift ministry. Prophets have insight by the Holy Spirit to pick up the winds of the Spirit. They hear what the Spirit is saying in various situations and nothing is hidden if God wants it enlightened. Often when a prophetic voice speaks to you, and it's accurate, you are left wondering: *How could they have known that?*

The point is that what you plan or say in your bedroom (out of the public eye), can be picked up by God's gift ministries when they operate under the anointing of the Spirit. Also what you say here is often an insight of what is really your heart. If your public desire is to do certain things in a particular way but it does not line up with what you say and feel privately, the likelihood of you succeeding then is very slim. The true heart will be achieved, not the one that people want to hear. If you believe you will fail behind closed doors, then it does not matter what you say in public. What you say at home and believe in your heart will surface in the way you behave. That is why it is crucial to know what God says about your circumstances because even in a recession when things shouldn't work, as long as you keep God's thinking alive in your spirit and declare the same behind closed doors, you will have what God indicated.

Gideon in **Judges 6** is a clear example of this concept in action. When the angel found him in a winepress at midnight, he was a man whose view of himself was the complete opposite of what God thought. God told him the truth. He was a mighty man of valour, **(Judges 6:12)** but through disappointments and not seeing what God had done previously for Israel in his current circumstances, he had become a cynic. Because he believed that God was no longer doing what he had been taught by his elders to believe, he had no faith to initiate any change in his situation. He was a man of valour and an instrument that God would use, but this is not how he saw himself. So his life of fear, doubt, and cynicism would continue until God intervened.

God was gracious and took him slowly through the phases of rebuilding his faith, until He got him to the place where what he now believed behind closed doors, was what was being said publically: **"The sword of the LORD and of Gideon." (Judges 7:20)** Victory was then imminent and his recovery, complete.

And since we have the same spirit of faith, according to what is written, "I believed and therefore I spoke," we also believe and therefore speak.
(2 Corinthians 4:13)

This is a recovery strategy that should be considered seriously. What happens to us in the process of life is not necessarily the final plan of God. We are definitely not what our circumstances dictate. I will produce fruit according to what I believe and what my experiences have been; therefore it is crucial in my recovery to allow God to develop in me what He sees. Declaring the word of God to me in faith and with expectation will eventually help me be renewed in the spirit of my mind. I will then produce the fruit of that changed image, regardless of my current situation. It's imperative that I believe who God says I am.

Jacob was a broken man after he had lost Joseph. Once he was unsure if Benjamin would return to him, he could endure no more. The spirit in Jacob was dead. But the words he heard that Joseph spoke, backed up by the provision he sent, resulted in his renewal: **"…the spirit of Jacob their father revived. Then Israel said, 'It is enough. Joseph my son is still alive. I will go and see him before I die.'" (Gen 45:27-28)** This can be your testimony as well. You may not see what God knows about you. But He knows the real you. Start to trust what He reveals to you, so that what you say in private will be seen in public.

Chapter Fifteen

THE BLESSING OF HONOURING GOD FIRST

And Elijah said to her, "Do not fear; go and do as you have said, but make me a small cake from it first, and bring it to me; and afterward make some for yourself and your son.

(1 Kings 17:13)

"But seek first the kingdom of God and His righteousness, and all these things shall be added to you."

(Matthew 6:33)

EXPERIENCE WHAT GOD CAN ADD TO YOU

Business kings, especially in tough financial seasons, should aim to be in a position where they connect with what God can **add** to their sales and general income figures. Whilst business kings have skill and anointing to generate income, sometimes they need a little extra from God to sustain them in prolonged difficult times. That is why it is very important to know God's financial principles, and what God can **add** to you. **(Matt 6:33)** It is especially important to be aware of the amazing principle of **honouring God first** because the reward will work in whatever economic climate is prevalent in the marketplace. Honour has within its ability the release of the miraculous. **(Mark 6:1-6)**

In the case of the widow in our scripture, she and her son had become the victims of a serious drought in the land and they had now reached the place of desperation. So much so, that she was on a final mission to gather a few sticks to make a fire to cook their last meal, before the inevitable. The only possible escape would be through divine intervention.

God sent Elijah across her path. He was a prophet on a specific mission at that moment. In fact she was the reason for him being there. God had already thought about her predicament and sent Elijah ahead to present her with an opportunity that would change her circumstances. Isn't it amazing to see that God sends 'spiritual gifting' to deal in natural environments? I must believe the same of God today. During my difficult economic times He has already released to me a solution. Instead of expecting the same problems and outcomes, I should learn from this example and train myself to look for what God has sent across my path to provide a solution for where I am. I need to look for the out of ordinary in my routine and establish whether this is God's hand in my situation.

It would seem very unusual or unfair for Elijah to arrive in the widow's life at that critical moment, and ask her to give him the **first** portion of their last meal. As a prophet of God who can hear the Spirit of God, one would assume that he would know what her predicament was, and move away from demanding a portion from the very little she still had; but this is exactly why Elijah was there. He was her answer from God. What he had would bring a breakthrough to her situation that she wasn't expecting. It required a decision, but it would result in saving her and her son's lives as well as the purpose of their household down the line.

It's never over in business or life until God says it is. You will always have more than a fighting chance to succeed in your tough economic seasons, if you are prepared to honour the principles of God **first**. God understood this widow's predicament, but feeling sorry for her or being emotional about where she was would not change the outcome. God still needed something to work with. Likewise, why would Jesus take a little boy's lunch? The little he had and offered up fed the multitude in the end, and the lad eventually went home with a lot more than he presented.

God needs something to work with to bring about miraculous changes. Elijah came into the widow's circumstances and asks her to give to him **first**. She made the decision to honour God's prophet as a first priority at that time, and because she put the things of God first, she and her son and their destiny as a family, lived way beyond the expectation their circumstances were suggesting. **(1 Kings 17:15-16)**

I believe many people in the church stay in the same circumstances because leaders struggle to challenge them to honour God first. It just seems so insensitive to ask them to give **first** to God when they have so little. Sentiment and emotion from leaders won't help people get out of where they are. Elijah wasn't insensitive. He knew exactly what their predicament was; but if he hadn't asked for the first slice of their last meal, (honour God first regardless) that family would have died and their destiny come to naught. Instead the widow's obedience led to supernatural provision in the hardest time of her life.

Always honour God with the best of your first. This is the stuff that creates **addition** to your finances.

HONORING GOD FIRST—EVEN WITH YOUR LAST

God needs to see your obedience and your willingness to obey Him, even if things appear hopeless. His Word has the power to produce life and change circumstances, and even those He sends to you have something to help change where you are. This widow held life and death in the balance. She had the choice of ignoring what this man of God was asking and remain focused on her plan of action.

So do we—Sunday after Sunday, the Word of God is preached all over the world and everyone who hears has that same choice. When God speaks to us, He wants it to profit us. He sends us His Word so that we can live and overcome in our situations.

> **For indeed the gospel was preached to us as well as to them; but the word which they heard did not profit them, not being mixed with faith in those who heard it.**

> **(Hebrews 4:2)**

Our widow thankfully chose life. She chose to believe the word of God delivered by Elijah. She saw him as a man of God, understood that God had sent him to them, and accepted that what he was saying was important, and responded by honouring God **FIRST.** She made sure God was in pole position in their predicament. She embraced and responded to His lifeline and in so doing, made room for God to do what He does. He rescues people and creates the evidence of the miraculous regardless of the current circumstances.

God must always be **first** in our operations and the way we conduct ourselves in life. Despite her personal circumstances, the widow was prepared to give **first** to God even from the **last** of what she had. This is a principle that business kings must learn. From what may appear to be their last, God must still get first. Your actions must show that regardless of your circumstances, you are still thinking about God and His honour. The **FIRST of your LAST** is also seed that can lead to an abundant, life-saving harvest that will sustain you in your economic crisis. Our widow discovered this. She ended up having provision throughout the very drought that had threatened their lives.

Recession is a modern form of drought. It is a financial famine—a drying up of cash flow and regular income – an uncertain market place and panic reactions in many quarters. It creates significant pressure and challenges the mindsets of business kings. What should I do here? What is the future now that this has arrived? But God is with you. He knows that drought and its severity is on the way. He knows that all in its path will be affected in some way. But God looks to help you. Perhaps the way He taught this principle to the widow seemed a little tough, but even though radical, it was her life-saver. Giving God the first of your even your last, is a miracle waiting to happen. It's not an emotional ploy. It's the way to change where you are. Be led of the Spirit. If He tells you to do this, obey as quickly as you can.

THE RESULT OF HER CHOICE

God **added** to her and kept her right through that intense time. Even though her circumstances were desperate, she saw to it that God was still her first priority. Her attitude is something God's kings can learn from. This is the type of person that would tithe off her gross salary and still give a tenth of her overall profit. She would make sure that what was God's got to Him and would leave instructions for her accountant where to place the monies in the business. She would be a **Proverbs 3:9-10** person, where she would give to God a tithe of all her increase and as a result have cash flow to do what her business required. She was guaranteed to have full barns and overflowing vats.

2 Kings 4:42-44 shows us this principle at work. A certain person brought his 'first fruit' offering of bread and set it before the people. The servant wondered how this little first fruit offering of bread would meet the needs of one hundred hungry men. God told him it was enough and there would also be leftovers.

Do you want your business to meet all its requirements and have leftovers as well? The secret lies in your approach and obedience to make sure that what belongs to God is a first priority to you. Our widow did exactly that and she **"ate for many days," (1 Kings 17:14-15)** where others in the nation had scraps and were preparing to die from starvation. When God sees business kings living in this way, where regardless of their circumstances they still look to God as a first priority, He will open up the windows of blessing for them. They have just shown Him that their circumstances are not more important than He is in their lives and supplies to sustain them are released from heaven. Money to them is proven to be just a tool and that God is the only focus of their heart.

These are important values when dealing in kingdom economics. All the while your mind screams at you, "Hold on to the little you have. Eat and you may have enough strength to last another day, and that could be when everything changes." But God says, "Give it me. I know how to multiply even the little you think is not important."

I am reminded of what Jesus said after He had shared the message of The Parable of the Sower: **"Therefore take heed how you hear. For whoever has, to him more will be given…" (Luke 8:18)**

Kings will live through economic recessions and last up to and beyond those times if they heed what they hear from the Spirit of God. What they hear can also come via the words of a person. But, however they hear, they need to quickly apply it to their business thinking and practices.

Chapter Sixteen

A LITTLE GOES A LOT FURTHER

**A certain woman of the wives of the sons
of the prophets cried out to Elisha, saying,
"Your servant my husband is dead, and
you know that your servant feared
the Lord. And the creditor is coming to
take my two sons to be his slaves."
So Elisha said to her, "What shall I do for
you? Tell me, what do you have in the
house?" And she said, "Your maidservant
has nothing in the house but a jar of oil."**

(2 Kings 4:1-2)

A COMMON THREAD IN BUSINESS

Sometimes in the difficult trading seasons the business
king's worst nightmare becomes a reality. Creditors come
for payments of accounts and you have insufficient cash
flow to deal with them. E-mails, letters from lawyers, and
ringing telephones never seem to stop reminding you of
what you owe and the terrible predicament you find
yourself in. There's no place to hide. No true king-in-
business for God ever really wants to be in such a position.
This is a pressure that is not welcome, but there are
unforeseeable times when this sadly does happen. Either it
has been introduced through world recession, collapsed
markets and credit systems, or self-induced through wrong
decision-making and negligent management of the

business. Whichever way it materializes it is not a good experience and it messes significantly with your stability and confidence as a financial king.

The widow was about to lose her sons in payment for her husband's business debts. They were about to be taken from her and they were the only means of future support available to her. Children are a heritage from God. Those who work in the business are able to go on and build the family line of success. Taking her sons in lieu of the debt is exactly what the devil would have attempted in order to destroy them as a family and put a stop to their financial destiny and heritage from God. Your business becoming stable and growing with generational purpose is certainly a threat to the kingdom of darkness.

Business kings will face these traumas of the marketplace occasionally and will have moments where you feel vulnerable and totally inadequate. These are times where you have to dig deep and know how to wage warfare for your businesses. This is not uncommon. Knowing how to be strong and decisive when things are tough in the marketplace must be a normal practice for God's kings-in-business.

When David's own mighty men turned on him to stone him, was one of these defining moments. **(1 Samuel 30)** He had to find a solution quickly. He had to be decisive in the way forward and **1 Samuel 30:6-8** shows what he did:

1) He strengthened himself in the Lord.
2) He asked for the ephod.
3) He inquired of the Lord.
4) He heard a rhema word from God.

REMEMBER WHAT YOU HAVE

So what is it that we can do in similar situations? Like David, we need to remember what we have already been given to use as a tool.

1. You have an anointing to destroy bondage

Isaiah 10:27 explains that it is the anointing of God that destroys the yoke of bondage. God has given you an anointing to be a business king in the marketplace. This anointing is more than adequate to deal with recession and cash flow problems that arise as a result. God is our source. This does not change. Respect what He has given to you. Guard it, protect it and release it to work in your situation. You have power to create wealth. **(Deut 8:18)** You have a capacity to make things work. Operate confidently in your anointing and watch with expectation how God will change things.

2. You have a mantle

2 Kings 2:13-15 shows that Elijah's mantle fell to the ground. Elisha picked it up and struck the waters of the Jordan River, dividing it in two parts. God has given you a particular mantle for the marketplace. You are anointed and well-equipped to strike the waters of the marketplace and forge a way of success in this economic arena. The business mantle God has given you is more than able to make you into a true king-in-business for Him. Pick up what God has given you and use it purposefully and confidently. Be fully persuaded in what God has enabled you to do. Strike the waters of your field of income with belief. Expect God to bless the work of your hands.

3. You have ability to be mentored

In **2 Kings 4:1**, the widow who approached Elisha had a husband who was connected to him, relationally. He was part of a group of prophets over which Elisha was a mentor. In reality she was planted and connected to a man of God in her city that was anointed to hear and speak the word of the Lord to any situation. Financial mentors are available to the body of Christ but business kings need to find them and sit under them, building trust in that relationship. The concept of being planted and becoming established is crucial to progress, especially in the financial realm. **(Psalm 92:12-15)** Being able to call on a man of God who has access to the Holy Spirit and the gift of the prophetic is a major plus for those in the marketplace. This is what the widow had, and it was the starting point of her recovery and ongoing success.

4. You have a recovery plan from God

In **2 Kings 4: 2-3** the widow only had a little oil in a jar, but she was in a position to gather many other empty vessels throughout her town. This is what we need to see: whilst everyone else had empty vessels lying around their homes, God then had an opportunity to multiply the little oil she had into those unused empty jars her neighbours were essentially holding in reserve for her. This was God's recovery plan for them as a family. BUT also, what God has given you personally as an anointing, has the potential to be given out and then resupplied so you have more with which to help others. God's recovery plan is that you are accelerated in your replenishment not only to pay your debts and have the rest to live on, but also to realize that the oil of anointing you carry is productive and evident, and needed by those around you. He wants them recovered as well.

Think about this apostolically. You may have something that God has given you, and many around you would benefit from the "oil" God has brought to your understanding. God imparts revelatory knowledge that equips you to radiate light and hope to those in need around you. These empty vessels would be transformed if the "oil" on your life and purpose were to reach them. Your church may have a revelation that others could enjoy and experience and would prove very helpful and prosperous to their situations. Think about the thousands of souls, for example, that have been brought into the kingdom through the Alpha courses now shared globally.

As the founder of Kings.net Ministries, I am not naïve to think that I have all the financial solutions for the church. I do know I have been raised as a father-figure to help churches as an apostle and give them the "oil" God has revealed to me in regards to the creation of finances for the kingdom. I am in a position to help pastors and business kings develop a working model that produces a release of wealth. God has revealed to me a strategy and synergy of gifting that works in the marketplace. This "oil" is able to fill the many empty vessels in the kingdom. So it is not for my use only. It can help replenish others as well.

5. You have a secret place to find God

2 Kings 4:5 reveals that you have a secret place to meet God behind closed doors. It's not only about having money or oil that others need. Your relationship with God and knowing how to lock yourself away with Him to hear the next download from heaven is crucial. It's more about enjoying fellowship with the One who is the resource and provider of the grace you have been allowed to discover. Waiting on God and being in His presence is as much of a financial king's lifestyle as the creating of the flow of finance into the kingdom. **(Psalm 91:1-2)**

The little you have is the seed of your personal recovery. Don't count yourself out because it appears so insignificant. A little in God's hands is all He needs to create your miracle.

Chapter Seventeen

PRECAUTIONS TO CONSIDER

**But also for this very reason, giving all
diligence, add to your faith virtue, to
virtue knowledge, to knowledge self-
control, to self-control perseverance, to
perseverance godliness, to godliness
brotherly kindness, and to brotherly
kindness love. For if these things are
yours and abound, you will be neither
barren nor unfruitful in the knowledge of
our Lord Jesus Christ. For he who lacks
these things is shortsighted, even to
blindness, and has forgotten that he was
cleansed from his old sins.
Therefore, brethren, be even more
diligent to make your call and election
sure, for if you do these things you will
never stumble.**

(2 Peter 1:5-10)

YOU WILL NOT STUMBLE

Peter teaches us here that there are certain attitudes and
behavioural traits that you can **add** diligently to your faith.
When you do, you strengthen your position to make your
call and election sure, creating a platform from where it is

difficult to stumble. Falling and even failing are real actualities in normal life, but there is a way to insure against those scenarios.

Consistently people and businesses experience defeat, loss, and failure and some of them crash very hard. Learning to deal with failure and setbacks in life should be a 'life-skill' subject taught in schools, because so much of this happens and people are ill prepared to handle them. Many people bare the scars of these encounters and carry huge emotional baggage, rendering them severely depleted in being able to rally and pick themselves up. Peter tells us here that there are things that we can practice and improve on, so we don't stumble. If you **add** certain traits to your lifestyle, you actually insure yourself against failure and the sense of stumbling around with nowhere to go.

What about the business world? Are there traits and principles that we can **add** to how we do business that will insure us against crashing out and failing?

PRACTICAL INSURANCE TIPS

1. Clarify always that God is your business resource.

Even though you have the skill and anointing to create wealth, **(Deut 8:18)** always acknowledge and depend upon God being the resource of your business. Avoid falling into the trap that 'you' are making things happen when all is going well. Abraham lifted his hand to God Most High and looked only to Him to create the wealth He had spoken about. **(Gen 14:22-23)** He was clearly focused so that no one else would get the glory, except God. When you read the context of **Deuteronomy 8**, the one concern God had of people attaining success was that their hearts could puff up and they could deceive themselves into thinking that it was their own skills or abilities that caused them to succeed. God would then be forgotten and fade out of the picture completely. **(Deut 8:7)**

God is clearly not opposed to His people succeeding in business, or life for that matter. He is apprehensive of the effect success is able to have on us. The illustration of a whale that someone once wrote fits here: *Just when you get to the top and start to blow, that's when you get harpooned.* Therefore, always see God as your resource—not your money, not your next amazing deal, not even the breakthrough client you have just landed. God alone is your provider. He alone is *Jehovah Jiheh* to your business. Depend on Him and come to Him with thanksgiving. Seek Him with humility for advice, direction, and blessing.

2. Honour God as the strength of your success.

Belshazzar saw what happened to his father Nebuchadnezzar when he acknowledged that *he* was the responsible for his own successes, and yet still did exactly the same as his father had done. God took Nebuchadnezzar's kingdom away from him **"…till he knew that the Most High God rules in the kingdom of men…" (Dan 5:21)** It was only returned to him when he accepted that the reason for his success was the God of Heaven. Belshazzar saw this **(Dan 5:22)** but still lifted himself up against the Lord of Heaven, praising rather the gods of silver, gold, bronze, iron, wood, and stone, ignoring the God who elevated him to a place of leadership and kingship. He turned away from the God who owned the power to hold his breath in His hand and all the successes of his ways. **(Dan 5:23)** When you allow that to happen, that is when the writing could appear on your wall. **(Dan 5:22-28)**

God is a jealous God and will not give His glory to another. Be quick to praise God and honour Him for His blessings and kindness. He is your only resource. This is a great insurance policy that will help you have major impact and success for God without the possibility of falling into pride and self-acclamation.

3. Be faithful in your local church.

A damaging distraction for a king-in-business is to miss regular fellowship with God, family, and church because of business pressure. There are going to be times when this is unavoidable and even necessary, but you need to guard against this occurring frequently and becoming a normal pattern in your relationship with God. These wiles of the devil sneak in almost unnoticeably, and when practiced sufficiently, they have the tendency to become habitual. **Psalm 92:12-15** reminds us of the importance of being planted in a local fellowship. It talks of flourishing **"...like a palm tree..."** and growing **"...like a cedar in Lebanon..."** tall and straight and standing above the rest. It also mentions bearing **"...fruit in old age..."** and being **"...fresh and flourishing."** The word *fresh* as used in this scripture means: *full of sap*. That's what we need to be as business kings for God and these are the fruits of being planted in your local church. This is worth adding. This insures you have a future.

4. Persevere—don't give up too soon.

It is sad but nevertheless true: so many people have missed all the best God has for them simply because they gave up too soon. Sometimes we have to pursue a little longer before we experience the breakthrough we desperately need. I heard someone preaching once and he used an illustration that I remember. (I can't remember whom the quote was from, but it stayed with me.) He said something along these lines, "The value of a postage stamp is seen in its ability to stick to the letter until it gets to its intended destination." Basically you need to stick to whatever it is God has shown you before you can arrive at the end result.

A danger to business kings is the need to always have quick returns. Sometimes the best returns take time to mature or find their way into being needed in the marketplace. The business king needs to know the value of his product, the season in the market place and whether he pulls out quickly or waits for things to turn.

Go back to your original purpose and the reasons you made when you decided to invest in the project. If its time is up, then end it quickly. The dilemma is to know what to do with certainty. Gideon's 300 men in **Judges 8:4** learned that despite exhaustion, the best plan for a return was to remain in pursuit, and as a result they reaped the rewards they set out to achieve.

Persevere with God and don't give up too early. Let God tell you it's time to pursue further, whether you are exhausted or not. Be careful to not let your emotions dictate what your next step should be. When the heat is turned up, it's not necessarily a sign that you pull out. Take David's advice in asking, **"'Shall I pursue this troop?'" (1 Sam 30:8)** He knew what it was to be under pressure and still be able to find out what God thought about his circumstances. This is a real key that can lead you into greater successes and increases in your business. God knows exactly where the fish are. Even though you may toil all night with little effect, Jesus told the disciples, **"'Cast the net on the right side of the boat, and you will find some.'" (John 21:6)** It is crucial to be able to hear what the Spirit of God is saying in your situation.

5. Observe basic business ethics.

Work hard. Nothing just happens for you to be successful. Show diligence in all you do. Everything matters—from the smallest, insignificant details to the largest ones. Your success depends also on the personal ethics you adopt to run your business practically. A casual attitude is an accident waiting to happen. Your business is a 24/7 endeavour. It needs your attention, your prayers, and your sensitivity to God. It demands that you are disciplined to its operating times, to keeping accurate accounts, to the payment of bills, and the handling of cash flow and the treatment of employees. Your mission statement must be clear and your business plan must be one that is current and workable.

Letting discipline slip makes room for larger indiscretions later on that could be your ruin. Be diligent with what God has given you. Remember the story of the talents in **Matthew 25**. The diligent servants got more from God and the one who achieved the most was rewarded with extra. The one who made excuses and buried his talent was rebuked and had to hand what he was given to the one who diligently produced the most. God observes your diligence with interest:

     a. **Proverbs 4:23 (Heart)**
     b. **Proverbs 12:24 (Hand)**
     c. **Proverbs 13:4 (Soul)**
     d. **Proverbs 21:5 (Plans)**

Don't be so spiritual that you are no earthly good. You must pray and seek God and be in a living relationship with Him, but you must also be able to practically work things on the ground. Praying for direction and then not being able to translate that into practical terms won't help you. There is a balance between the spiritual and the practical. You will need both understandings. It is always wise in life to remember an old saying, "Take care of the pennies and they will take care of the pounds." Pay diligent attention to the practical details, no matter how small they are, and that will help you attend adequately to the larger ones. Success in business needs the understanding of God's economics and the implementation of solid, disciplined, and practical business ethics.

Chapter Eighteen

FAIR PLAY

Let the elders who rule well be counted worthy of double honor, especially those who labor in the word and doctrine. For the Scripture says, "You shall not muzzle an ox while it treads out the grain," and, "The laborer is worthy of his wages."

(1 Timothy 5:17-18)

FINANCIAL CHURCH BOARDS AND WAGES

It has changed for the better in more recent years, but when I started out in ministry, it felt as if certain people controlled everything and that the sent 'gift ministry' worked for these individuals. I often felt I was not free to lead the congregation on the path I believe God had for it because my future was threatened if I did not follow suit. Sadly, some of these people were moneyed people and been at the church forever, and I often struggled with feelings of being under their control. It felt like I was the visitor and needed to come into their line! Church politics has been the cause of much heartache for full-time ministers and members alike, and not getting this balance right can lead to much pain, mistrust and unnecessary confusion in the church. I believe that those who administrate the funds should do it with understanding of the value of the gift man God has sent, and as a blessing, not allowing themselves to feel they need to be in control of what happens. There needs to be ordered control and budgets that are monitored by the leader and financial team but never a manipulation because someone controls the purse. Each local church must endeavor to have a Godly financial structure in place, where the monitoring of funds available is carried out with all fairness, righteousness and peace.

God didn't hold back when it came to saving mankind. He took the best He had in heaven – His only Son – and gave Him to the world. It cost God everything to offer us a plan of salvation. What price can you affix to such a sacrifice?

When it comes to paying employees in business, God watches the scales and balances employers apply. God loves generosity. He loves when employers make just decisions to honour and pay staff exactly what they are worth, and refrain from looking for ways to keep money from them.

> **Come now, you rich, weep and howl for your miseries that are coming upon you! Your riches are corrupted, and your garments are moth-eaten. Your gold and silver are corroded, and their corrosion will be a witness against you and will eat your flesh like fire. You have heaped up treasure in the last days. Indeed the wages of the laborers who mowed your fields, which you kept back by fraud, cry out; and the cries of the reapers have reached the ears of the Lord of Sabaoth.**
>
> **(James 5:1-4)**

This scripture is not saying, "The Lord of the SABBATH." The cries come before "The Lord of SABAOTH" or the Lord of Hosts who is in charge of the warring angelic beings that fight on behalf of God's plans of justice for His people. It is not wise to have unfair and fraudulent cries reaching The Lord of Sabaoth. Instead, God will honour the businesses that treat their staff fairly and don't exploit them in any way. In our opening scripture, Timothy taught that those Pastors who rule well should be noted and counted worthy of double honour. Make sure you are a king-in-business that desires to see your set man honoured and not frustrated through lack of finances, especially if they are being withheld from him. In many ways he is like an ox, labouring tirelessly to bring you the grain from heaven. This gift should not be muzzled financially. This is the way God feels about those who operate diligently in a full-time capacity in the ministry. They are worth double pay.

UNFAIR SCALES

Jacob came to work for Laban in **Genesis 29** and the experience he had presents a picture of the type of employer that should be avoided. Firstly, he asked Jacob, **"Tell me, what should your wages be?" (Gen 29:15)** Jacob replied that he would serve seven years for Rachel, his younger daughter. **(v18)** Jacob did this and when it was time for Laban to honour the agreement, he deceived Jacob into marrying the eldest daughter and work another seven years for Rachel. Secondly, Laban changed his wages ten times. **(Gen 31:7)** One of the greatest faults with employers today that are a cause of deep hurts in people, are employers who mislead their employees by promising them things they never intended to give them. They are selfish exploiters of defenseless people who are dependent on their employers for sustenance. These employers are in a place of authority and power to control or manipulate those under them. God watches the scales they use when dealing with those they have authority over. It would be prudent to remember what the centurion, who spoke to Jesus about his sick servant, understood. He was in a place of power to rule and command because of his position and rank, but understood well that he was also under the power and authority of another. God is the Business King's authority. We are under Him and so we should be very fair and just when it comes to dealing with those dependent on us.

JEHOVAH GMOLAH

What employers should also remember is that one of the covenant names of God is **"Jehovah Gmolah,"** meaning, "the Lord my compensation." God is just and therefore a lover of justice, fairness, and righteous dealings. He will make sure that His people, who have been short changed and not compensated fairly, will get what has been kept from them. Even if it doesn't appear to be immediate, His fairness and justice will eventually bring a full compensation. It would be important then to know:

1) **The Lord rewarded me according to my righteousness; According to the cleanness of my hands He has recompensed me. (Ps 18:20)**

2) **"Restore all that was hers, and all the proceeds of the field from the day that she left the land until now." (2 Kings 8:6)**

3) **A man will be satisfied with good by the fruit of his mouth, And the recompense of a man's hands will be rendered to him. (Prov 12:14)**

4) **According to their deeds, accordingly He will repay, Fury to His adversaries, Recompense to His enemies;**

168

The coastlands He will fully repay. (Isa 59:18)

5) **"Vengeance is Mine, and recompense;**
   Their foot shall slip in due time;
   For the day of their calamity is at hand"
   (Deut 32:35)

In the case of Jacob with Laban, where he was cheated and lied to repeatedly, God made sure Jacob left fully compensated for the time he had given in labour. Although the time spent with Laban was a real challenge to Jacob personally (God was dealing with his character issues as well), when he left Laban to return home, he was not empty-handed. He was well-compensated for the time spent there. A warning is issued here for the Laban's of the business world: The time will come when you stand to lose what you think you have. God gave Jacob a plan to multiply his own wealth from Laban's stock, and this was with Laban's permission. The results were amazing;

> **Thus the man became exceedingly**
> **prosperous, and had large flocks, female**
> **and male servants, and camels and**
> **donkeys.**
>
> **(Genesis 30:43)**

God is a God of compensation. He let Jacob encounter the dealings of another swindler of note (Laban) and used the experience to change Jacob's character; but when the time of completion arrived, Jacob left a very prosperous man. God compensated Israel as well for serving the Egyptians for 430 years. He arranged for the Egyptians to give them gold, silver, and clothing as they were leaving. The scripture records it this way, **"...So you shall plunder the Egyptians."** (Exod 3:22)

God is abundantly fair and looks to see where people in authority over others, are the same. Moses was instructed to tell Israel how to conduct their affairs in the Promised Land in Deuteronomy 15. The chapter deals with releasing those in debt after seven years, and how to treat the poor brother in their midst. He said, **"You shall surely give to him and your heart should not be grieved when you give to him, because for this thing the Lord your God will less you in all your works and in all to which you put your hand….You shall not let him go away empty-handed."** **(Deut 15:10, 13)** Without fail we can see the heart God has for those who struggle and how pleased He is with those who freely give to help and be fair to those who have nothing.

Let this serve as an encouragement to God's kings who have employees: be to them as God is to us. Be just, be fair, and be honest. Have your scales checked so they balance correctly. Always play fair with others who are seemingly at your mercy. Their whole livelihood depends on your fairness. God looks for this in people who have this authority and HE rewards you by BLESSING whatever your hands find to do.

Chapter Nineteen

SPEAKING BLESSING AS A TOOL

Now behold, Boaz came from Bethlehem,
and said to the
reapers, "The Lord be with you!"
And they answered him, "The Lord bless
you!"

(Ruth 2:4)

Then he stood and blessed all the
assembly of Israel with a loud voice,
saying: "Blessed be the Lord, who has
given rest to His people Israel, according
to all that He promised. There has not
failed one word of all His good promise,
which He promised through His servant
Moses. May the Lord our God be with us,
as He was with our fathers. May He not
leave us nor forsake us, that He
may incline our hearts to Himself, to walk
in all His ways, and to keep His
commandments and His statutes and His
judgments, which He commanded our
fathers. And may these words of mine,
with which I have made supplication
before the Lord, be near the Lord our
God day and night, that He may maintain
the cause of His servant and the cause of

His people Israel, as each day may
require, that all the peoples of the earth
may know
that the Lord is God; there is no other..."

(1 Kings 8:55-60)

On the eighth day he sent the people
away; and they blessed the king, and went
to their tents joyful and glad of heart for
all the good that the Lord had done for
His servant David, and for Israel His
people.

(1 Kings 8:66)

Then Joseph brought in his father Jacob
and set him before Pharaoh; and
Jacob blessed Pharaoh.

(Genesis 47:7)

BASIC INSIGHTS INTO BLESSING

In Chapter Four of this book, I spoke about the synergy of
the Prophet – Priest – King (in business) as an ancient,
established path for the people of God. This is a strategy
that ensures financial blessing through the synergy of gift
ministries. Being ancient should not be interpreted as old,
archaic, or out of date; and therefore have little to offer.
Those who grasp the revelation of **BLESSING** and
SPEAKING BLESSING will get to experience the effects
of God's goodwill intentions being sown into the difficult
and unfruitful areas of their lives and get to enjoy the
power that these blessings create in places where little hope
was expected. Blessing was practiced as far back as the
days of the patriarchs and is still alive today for those who
will believe and embrace its truth.

And the Lord spoke to Moses,
saying: "Speak to Aaron and his sons,
saying, 'This is the way you shall bless the
children of Israel. Say to them:
"The Lord bless you and keep you;
The Lord make His face shine upon you,
And be gracious to you;
The Lord lift up His countenance upon
you,
And give you peace."'
"So they shall put My name on the
children of Israel, and I will bless them."

(Numbers 6:22-27)

After leaving Egypt, the very first assembled priesthood
(Aaron and his sons), was instructed by God to **bless** the
people in a particular way. God made it clear that the duties
of the priests needed to include the release of the **spoken
blessings** into their circumstances. Such is the power and
potential that this blessing contains. This was a command
of God to the priests. God wanted them to release the
power that 'blessing' had into their situations so that they
could benefit and progress and not be dominated by their
circumstances.

As a business king for God, we have to deal with the
marketplace and its uncertainties and pressures. Knowing
that where we are planted, there is a PRIEST, who
understands this revelation and speaks the blessing over my
business regularly, would be very comforting. This release
of blessing is part of the priest's God-given anointing and
when anointing is present, **"…the yoke will be destroyed
because of the anointing oil." (Isa 10:27)** Nothing can
hinder the anointing of God that is released to a situation.
This function of the priest is part of the gift package that

makes up the synergy in the Prophet—Priest—King strategy. The release of spoken blessing is a great asset to the business kings in the kingdom. The value these Kings-in-business place on their priests is therefore crucial.

THE VALUE OF RELEASING BLESSING

Blessing was part of Israel's culture. It started with God declaring it as His intention to creation. **(Gen 1:28)** In time, it became quite normal for Israel to release the language of blessing. We see in scripture that the whole language mindset of Israel, was interwoven with thoughts of releasing blessing:

> **Neither let those who pass by them say,**
> **"The blessing of the Lord be upon you;**
> **We bless you in the name of the Lord!"**

> **(Ps 129:8)**

> **As he loved cursing, so let it come to him;**
> **As he did not delight in blessing, so let it**
> **be far from him.**
> **(Ps 109:17)**

Blessing was a huge factor in Israel's history. By the time of Esau, the power and fruitfulness of the blessing was already an expectation. When Esau realized that he had lost the **firstborn blessing**, he was completely distraught and overcome, crying unashamedly and pleading for his father to have at least another blessing in reserve for him. **(Gen 27:34-38)** Israel had grasped and begun to use this amazing concept with powerful results. When Jacob was on his deathbed he called his sons together and spoke a specific blessing to each one:

**All these are the twelve tribes of Israel,
and this is what their father spoke to
them. And he blessed them; he blessed
each one according to his own blessing.**

(Gen 49:28)

Peter tells us that part of New Testament life is also to
embrace blessing as a concept:

**Finally, all of you be of one mind, having
compassion for one another; love as
brothers, be tenderhearted, be
courteous; not returning evil for evil or
reviling for reviling, but on the
contrary blessing, knowing that you were
called to this, that you may inherit a
blessing.**

(1 Peter 3:8-9)

The first opportunity Joseph had to have his children
blessed came when he was reunited with the family in
Egypt. When Jacob saw Joseph's sons, the first action in
his mind was to ask permission to bless them. **(Gen 48:8-9)**

In order to validate the importance of the release of the
spoken blessing to the church today, I have outlined briefly
what I call, "The Firsts of Blessing" as they appear in the
Word of God.

1) **Genesis 1:28** The first words God spoke to us in Adam.

2) **Genesis 5:2** The first words God spoke to mankind in
   their genealogy.

3) **Genesis 47:7-10** The first greeting Jacob had with Pharaoh.

4) **Genesis 48:8-9** The first interaction of Jacob with Joseph's sons.

5) **Genesis 49:28** The first mention of a father's blessing to his children.

6) **Numbers 6:22-27** The instruction to the first priesthood, post-Egypt.

7) **Ruth 2:4** The first blessing to employees.

8) **Matthew 5** The first message of Jesus to a crowd.

9) **Mark 10:16** The first child that sat on Jesus's lap.

10) **Luke 2:34** The first words Simeon spoke to Joseph and Mary.

The value of speaking and releasing blessing can also be measured by some final comments that were mentioned. The words of Jesus to His disciples just prior to His ascension into heaven were words of blessing. **(Luke 24:50-51)**

There is so much evidence of the value that this concept has in the lives of God's people, that to ignore it would be just wrong. God has placed in our grasp a tool that has power to create miraculous changes to the circumstances of our lives. Why would we not want to learn how to use it?

USING BLESSING IN BUSINESS

We catch a glimpse of this practice in the business arena in **Ruth 2**. Boaz, the owner of the land and financial king in those times, was returning home from a business trip. It was the time of the harvest. All his employees were busy harvesting his crop. When Boaz came onto his lands and walked over his fields and saw workers, he greeted them saying, **"The Lord be with you."** (v4) This was similar to the greeting the angel spoke to Mary in **Luke 1:28** and to Gideon in **Judges 6:12**. These greetings contained a message of hope and encouragement. Mary was to be blessed among women as she was chosen to be the mother of Jesus and Gideon was called a mighty warrior enabled to do the bidding of the Lord in conquering Israel's enemies. Literally when you greeted people in this way you were implying that God, by His presence, be with you to comfort, refresh, empower, and assist you in your tasks ahead. To have this spoken over you by your employer consistently, brought to your understanding that he wanted to see God enable and channel success towards you. He desired to see you prospering and experiencing increase.

As we learn more about the significance of what blessing actually meant, the greeting Boaz received in return is a tool that businesses should encourage and understand. The word *bless* or *to release blessing* has its foundation in the act of a person kneeling before God, with hands lifted up, and in submission and worship of the Most High God. A believer kneels before this powerful, majestic, and Holy God and blesses Him. It's a picture of the lesser one in adoration of the One who is above all. It also carries with it some derivative meanings for us that are helpful in understanding how to speak and apply this blessing in our situations. Speaking 'blessing' also meant to:

1) Empower you to succeed
2) Prosper you
3) Release favour upon you
4) Benefit you
5) Add value to you

6) Make you like a gift

7) Unlock to you what suits your purpose

So when the reapers saw Boaz and received his blessing spoken to them, they replied, **"The Lord bless you!" (Ruth 2:4)** What they were releasing over his life was in fact: *God empower you to succeed in your task as a landowner, business king and one of influence in our community. May He add value to you and cause you to be a benefit to His purpose, having favour find you and anointing on your calling so that you accomplish exactly all you were born to do.*

This practice in the marketplace amongst God's business kings would increase the potential of healthy business returns. Owners, who want God's intervention and presence with their workers where they are enabled and assisted by God to do their level best for the company, should release this goodwill blessing over them consistently. What you tap into and believe God for will eventually manifest where you are. Your workers will come to know the blessing of God's leading and presence as a reality. This will be good for business when this sort of anointing is released.

On the other hand, when they reply, **"The Lord bless you!" (Ruth 2:4)** they are inviting and entreating God to cause you, as a business owner, to operate with a level of success that would be a blessing and benefit to you and add value to you as a business king in the area. People would see the favour of God on you and the depth of blessing that exists. When the workers pray and speak this blessing over their employer that is a basis for good business returns. They desire God's goodness to be with you in your decision-making and want the success He has in mind for you. This benefits your sales in the marketplace and your success keeps the business afloat and your workers in a position to have regular increases and consistent employment.

For what it's worth, I have practiced this concept on a group of business kings for more than ten years now. For the most part, their businesses have grown and excelled and maintained their courses, even in lean times. They have felt the pressure of the uncertain and collapsed markets, but they are still standing today. Sadly, some have struggled and continue to do so, but there are reasons for this. The Word of God always works, but sometimes we are a little slow at embracing its truth and often only spring into action when the horse has already bolted. Those that have placed themselves under the revelatory teaching of the Word of God and accepted its principles for the marketplace have a story to tell. The anointing oil breaks the yoke of bondage. Financial kings must position themselves accordingly for success. Famine and drought are tough seasons in the financial kingdom, but they don't have to be devastating to you. Take advantage of what God has made available for your success:

1) A **calling** for marketplace function, and an anointing to succeed.
2) The presence of the **Holy Spirit** to lead and guide your decision-making.
3) The advantage of **choice prophets** releasing and confirming your now words from God in the correct timing.
4) **Priests** who speak and release the language and concept of blessing to your purpose in the marketplace.
5) **Financial mentors** that stir your hearts of faith for God with revelatory insights to inspire your personal kingship anointing.

6) A **promise of growth** from God even in the winter seasons. **(Ps 65:10)**

The markets and where they are on the world's scale don't really determine if you should or could succeed—God does. He is your resource. His methods have worked in all seasons and continue to do so. They have stood the test of time and still work today as they were intended. The release of blessing is a tool that we must embrace again with all earnestness. Blessing has within it the goodwill intentions of God that will be able to create change in your stagnant unproductive areas.

The language of blessing is a powerful arrow in the business king's quiver.

Chapter Twenty

THE SIGNIFICANCE OF YOUR PURPOSE

In the eighteenth year of his reign, when he had purged the land and the temple, he sent Shaphan the son of Azaliah, Maaseiah the governor of the city, and Joah the son of Joahaz the recorder, to repair the house of the Lord his God.

(2 Chronicles 34:8)

A COMPONENT OF THE REPAIR TEAM

All through the Word of God you will find references to **Prophet – Priest – King** combinations and it's the synergy of these gift ministries that creates a powerful anointing for success in the marketplace arena. Business kings already have skills and abilities given by God, but when you add the dimension of the prophetic and priestly ministries, you surround the marketplace gift with words of confirmation, direction, or warning as well as the spoken blessings released by the set man, who is anointed with this mantle.

For example, when the temple needed to be repaired, young King Josiah from our foundational scripture above, sent **three** people to begin the process. In Old Testament times there was huge significance placed on the appearance of the physical temple. Its physical state was a picture of the value and importance the people placed on the God they worshipped there. It's no accident that the three people sent to repair the building were a combination of the Prophet – Priest – King gifting. Other places in scripture where you find this synergy and become aware of their value can also be found:

1) **Genesis 14:18-20**
2) **Exodus 17: 8-15**
3) **1 Kings 4:1-7**
4) **2 Kings 19:2-3**
5) **Haggai 1:1**

Taking this thought into the New Testament, we are no longer required to have beautiful, physical buildings before the validity of God can be seen or experienced. We are the temple today. Christ in us is the hope of glory. Sometimes the best picture people will have of a living Jesus is the picture we present to them. Still, this synergy of **Prophet – Priest – King** is relevant for the ongoing success of the church today. It is the dimension, that in my belief, the church really needs to rethink. The church is not a business as such. It is a place for the lost and broken to find Jesus and a new life in Him. But the church does require finance to be operational and successful. This is the king-in-business's function. He needs to operate in his anointing to bring the wealth of the world into the church so that it does not suffer lack in reaching the lost and being effective in the local communities. Business kings are a component of God's repair team. He surrounds them with prophetic input (prophets) and spoken blessing (priests) so that they can enjoy success in the marketplace. (See story of Joshua in **Exodus 17:8-15**.) As long as Moses had his arms raised with open hands over Joshua and the army in the valley,

Israel was able to move victoriously forward. But the prophet (Moses) had to have his arms held up by a priest (Aaron) and a business king (Hur) before Joshua succeeded. This is a banner that churches need to reinstate in their ranks. Their business kings should experience the benefit of this three-fold banner just as Joshua did. Kings that succeed in the marketplace allow the church financial freedom to complete its mission to a lost and dying world.

Business kings need to look carefully for recovery principles in this portion of the Word of God. **(Exodus 17)** For example:

1) Moses spoke to Joshua and said, **"Choose us some men and go out, fight with Amalek." (v9)** Moses (the prophet in this synergy) was saying *we are together in this. You being in the valley is not an indication that it is not my battle as well. You are part of the team and your function in the valley* (marketplace) *is just as important as mine on the top of this mountain.*

2) When Moses went up to his position he was accompanied by a priestly and kingly gifting. An under banner was shown as the way to proceed successfully in the market place. Modern day business kings should be covered similarly. Observe how these gift ministries supported Moses to ensure that Joshua overcame in the valley. **(v10-12)**

3) God then said to Moses to **"Write this for a memorial in the book and recount it in the hearing of Joshua..." (v14)** God wanted us to remember the significance of this victory and He

especially wanted Joshua to know how he won the
battle in the valley with Amalek. It was
accomplished through the result of God's
breakthrough strategy…Prophet – Priest –
King…working in synergy. It is a picture of the
repair team that needs to be reassembled today,
particularly in the financial arena.

God has a repair team today for the state of the church's
finances. The church does not normally lack anointing,
worshippers, pastors or leaders, but many do lack adequate
finance to fulfill God-given visions. Insufficient finances
are the cry of many potentially significant churches and
works of God. The business king needs to see himself as
part of this vital ministry repair team or begin the
groundwork to make sure it is established in his ranks.

UNDERSTAND THE AMALEK SPIRIT

You will notice that Amalek came and fought with Israel at
Rephidim. **(v8)** Rephidim means *rests* and Amalek is
translated to show that it is *a warlike spirit*. His whole
modus operandi was to attack when the other party was at
rest, or inactive. He would sneak up to ambush, amputate
and leave the opposition maimed and severely destroyed. It
didn't stay in the financial arena only, but spilled over into
lives, purposes and destinies of people, family and
circumstances. It is a crippling, fierce and horrible ploy of
the enemy against God's people.

Kings-in-business particularly need to be aware of these
tactics when they are regrouping and getting ready to move
to another level in financial impact in the marketplace.
While you are seemingly at rest, the attack comes to keep
you at that place where you have rested. The plan is that
you don't progress further than you have come. No wonder

God wanted that spirit annihilated. So many business kings get attacked in this manner. They feel stopped before they go anywhere. Kings need to take this spirit into account to maintain recovery and advancement.

PUT GOD IN REMEMBRANCE

Isaiah 43:26 encourages us to put God in remembrance of His Word. We should remind God that we are holding on to His Word over us; that we are waiting expectantly for what has been prophesied or given as a rhema word (a now word) that cannot return void, nor can the gates of hell prevail against them. Remind the Lord that you believe His prophets and therefore you will prosper in the task He has allocated for you. The Psalmist says,

> **Remember the word to Your servant,**
> **Upon which You have caused me to hope.**
> **This is my comfort in my affliction,**
> **For Your word has given me life.**
>
> **(Ps 119:49-50)**

Prayerfully remind God that He has called and appointed you as a business king in the marketplace—a provider, a conduit of financial blessing—one that has the anointing to transfer the wealth of the world into the purposes of the kingdom. Therefore you are trusting in His favour and kindness to allow opportunities to come your way so that your call will be established. Share with God the delight you have in this ministry calling and how important it is for you to fulfill all He has required. Call on God and believe Him to move and bless your business and bring it to a significant place of growth and productivity. Share with God that you desire to get to where Solomon's financial governors arrived at, where **"…there was no lack in their supply." (1 Kings 4:27)** These governors each had a part in financing the palace's needs for one calendar month, whilst they attended to their own businesses as well. They succeeded with the testimony that there was no lack in their ministry purpose. What had been required of them was more than adequately met.

Voice prayerfully and confidently your faith expectations. You are in business for God, so succeed in your call. You are not there to fail. Difficult times and market pressures come to all in this field. You do feel this heat. When these struggles arrive and recovery is required, there is nothing more rewarding than to remember who appointed you and what He has already spoken over you. **"God is not a man, that He should lie." (Num 23:19)** What He has called and appointed you to, He is well able to complete. Your present circumstances do not determine who you are. Joseph found himself in an Egyptian slave market being sold as a slave. At this point, the dream God had given him was nowhere near what he was experiencing. Yet the Word says that God was with him and he was successful. **(Gen 39:2)** God didn't ignore him or leave him in that state of disregard.

You are on course to be successful in the marketplace. God is working all things for the good. He is with you. Believe in and value the ability your anointing carries. God always completes what He begins.

Chapter Twenty-One

ASSURING YOU HAVE LEFTOVERS

**Then a man came from Baal
Shalisha, and brought the man of God
bread of the first fruits, twenty loaves of
barley bread, and newly ripened grain in
his knapsack. And he said, "Give it to the
people, that they may eat."
But his servant said, "What? Shall I set
this before one hundred men?"
He said again, "Give it to the people, that
they may eat; for thus says
the Lord: 'They shall eat and have some
left over.'"**

(2 Kings 4:42-43)

OPPORTUNITY TO CREATE LEFTOVERS

The list is endless. There are many reasons why businesses
fail or find they need to recover. There are both practical
and spiritual reasons for this. Now it is true that there are
millions of businesses out there that are not in touch with

God at all, and yet are successful. But when something goes wrong with them for example and their level of expertise runs dry, they don't have much to fall back on. They are unaware of how to find solutions from God. Some spiritually-owned businesses fail because that is for the most part all they have. Spiritual know-how with little practical knowledge is extremely dangerous, but at least this group has God to fall back on and His resources are unlimited.

A combination of sound, practical business know-how, coupled with mature Godly counsel and Word of God knowledge, are the ingredients for ongoing success. As business kings for God, you must understand the merit of obedience to the principles that govern God's financial economic strategy. Just like God has principles that govern the concepts of love, forgiveness, sin, and salvation, He has principles that work in the area of finances. It is not wise to only have some knowledge of these principles. **Knowledge** with **understanding** paves the way for **wisdom** to prevail. Wisdom is the proper application of the knowledge of God. Where these operate, success will follow. Recovery will be imminent. Being diligent and obedient to knowing God's economic structures, coupled with practical business sense, is what is required.

In the portion of scripture I have chosen to introduce this chapter, there is a reference to **leftovers** connected to **first fruits**. Giving your **first** of the **best** you have to God, is what Abel did in **Genesis 4:4** and it earned high praise from God. Abel's sacrifice was chosen above Cain's. The giving of your first to God reveals the truth that even the portion left after you have honoured the principle of first fruits to God, will also abound in God's blessing. The whole batch will be considered holy to God. **(Rom 11:16)** The blessing that first fruits create will spread like leaven through the whole deal. It will be able to support and

188

finance what is required and have the added bonus of the promise of leftovers. God makes sure that what is left after first fruits, is anointed and increased sufficiently to handle the whole cost of what is still required. It's a similar concept to God making the nine tenths of your pay cheque handle the full month's financial necessities after your tithe is paid. How He does it and the way it's done cannot be explained. But He does it every time. When all bills are met, what is left over creates the cash flow that will help finance the next deal. The more cash flow my business has on hand, the less I have to borrow with interest from the bank.

THE PROMISE OF LEFTOVERS

A keynote to financial recovery is to make sure that what was increase to your deal, has God's **fat** separated and brought to the storehouse as a **first fruit**. Always make sure God is honoured with what belongs to Him. The book of Proverbs has some exciting advice to offer:

> **Honor the Lord with your possessions,**
> **And with the first fruits of all your**
> **increase;**
> **So your barns will be filled with plenty,**
> **And your vats will overflow with new**
> **wine.**

> **(Proverbs 3:9-10)**

Every business would love to see filled barns and overflowing vats and this scripture shows us the way to achieve this. Honouring God with your possessions— separating the first fruits of your increase—creates this blessing. To ignore this is just not wise. You must know what is profitable to your business and then calculate the tithe that belongs to God. When God sees His business kings with this heart He will make sure that their barns are full and there is healthy overflow (cash flow) for the business to operate further. This is a good place at which to arrive. Cash flow means there are no debts and therefore no pressure from the banking world or investors.

God wants us blessed in life with adequate resources to meet our basic needs. Jesus taught that we would always have the poor with us, but that was not an indication that it was normal and acceptable to struggle and live below the bread line. If we were meant to be poor, why is there so much opportunity to increase and prosper? Why does God not just tell us that He wants us to be poor and to struggle? No, working with and honouring God's financial principles will increase your level of blessing, relatively. Even those with little financial fortitude will benefit from their obedience to the word of God on finances. When God told Israel to test Him in this, **(Mal 3:10)** the merits of this obedience abounded unbelievably. It spanned the concepts of protection, provision, and favour. God didn't select a particular race, colour, creed, or income level status as a starting point. The word was to all, despite where people were situated.

To be blessed or prosperous means you have enough for your needs and the needs of your family, and you have some **left over** with which to be a blessing to those around you. Jesus demonstrated the concept of having leftovers several times. In the miracle of feeding the 5,000 **(Matt 14:15-20)** and then also the 4,000 **(Matt 15:32-39)** there were twelve and seven baskets of leftovers, respectively. All in attendance were completely satisfied. No one was hungry and left wanting more. This shows clearly that when God provides and we are obedient, there is always more than enough to meet the need. The evidence of leftovers proves this desire of God for the prospering of His people. **(2 Kings 4:43)**

There is no thought of lack or a struggling budget with God. The widow with the little jar of oil left in her house followed the instructions of the Prophet Elisha and had more than enough **leftovers** to not only pay her husband's business debts, but also had enough for herself and her sons to live on. **(2 Kings 4:7)** Her obedience led to **leftovers** that stretched way beyond what she could have imagined. This is part of God's plan for your recovery.

God wants us to have leftovers. This is a good fruit to cultivate when in business.

Chapter Twenty-Two

VALLEY RECOVERY

**Then a man of God came and spoke to the
king of Israel, and said, "Thus says
the Lord: 'Because the Syrians have said,
"The Lord is God of the hills, but
He is not God of the valleys," therefore I
will deliver all this great multitude into
your hand, and you shall know that
I am the Lord.'"**

(1 Kings 20:28)

HILLS AND VALLEYS

It's a wonderful feeling when business is going great and
everything is on a high. Sadly there are moments and
difficulties when the down times are around and things in
business can be awfully quiet and very uncertain. These
valley experiences are challenging and can make their mark
on God's business kings. The **highs** are great and always
wanted, but that is not always the ongoing norm.

God had some advice for Israel after they had inflicted a
great victory over the Syrians. They were on a tremendous
high and very upbeat about their progress. God spoke to
them and encouraged them to strengthen themselves and
prepare again, for the Syrians would be back at the turn of
the season.

**And the prophet came to the king of
Israel and said to him, "Go, strengthen
yourself; take note, and see what you
should do, for in the spring of the year the
king of Syria will come up against you."**

(1 Kings 20:22)

In other words, use this time to prepare yourself for another
attack. They will be back again. Don't be carried away with
your win, trying to maintain the feeling of the high that you
have experienced. We don't live from one mountaintop to
another. Two main thoughts emerge here for business
kings:

1) Always prepare for further victory, as well as the
   defense of your winning position. You have to carve out
   a winning profile and work at it until it functions
   regularly and consistently. When you play against sports
   teams that win most of the time it's harder to defeat
   them, because they have developed a "winning culture."
   Part of maintaining this winning culture is to ensure that
   you visit your defense mechanisms as well, and don't
   overplay your victory time. Praise God for His hand of
   blessing and favour. Prepare to defend what you have
   won. Your enemy knows how he lost and is devising a
   move to defeat your game plan.

2) Build into your mind-set that God is not only the God of
   the hills, but also God in your valley experiences. There
   are times you will lose in the overall battle. This is when
   your faith must arise in God who has shown that He is
   master of your valley times as well.

194

VALLEY ENCOURAGEMENTS

Scripture offers us many examples of God's provision in the valley times that could serve as encouragement for a king-in-business.

1. The valley of ditches (2 Kings 3:16)

Through wrong alliances with ungodly family (Ahab and Jezebel), King Jehoshaphat ended up in a dangerous situation. He had agreed to go with Ahab into battle, and en route to their battleground, because they didn't make room for Godly council, found they had gone on a roundabout route and arrived at the place where their water was depleted and they had none to give the soldiers or the livestock. All the mechanics of waging a successful campaign were now in jeopardy because of severe thirst and dehydration beginning to settle in over the force. Being unequally yoked is a real danger in business. God needs to be a real lead in your business and if that relationship is absent, you cut yourself off from Godly leadership and direction just as Jehoshaphat had.

However God came through for them when they decided to find Elisha (a prophet of God) and seek a word of direction for their situation. It's imperative for business kings to hear and seek the counsel of God for their recovery. It's not negotiable. It's absolutely crucial. God revealed immediately that He was God in their personal valley experience. Elisha told them to **dig ditches** (water canals) throughout the whole valley they were in and God would fill them with the water supply they needed.

Even in this place of near capitulation, God had an answer—a way out for them. God has an answer for you as well. You first have to make room for God to release His provision. What are you releasing to 'catch' what God wants to send? You may not see or understand how He will rescue you or do what He has said. That is not the point. Your obedience and trust will create the miracle your valley requires.

You must be seeking God and inquiring, "What exactly is the 'water' that will lead to my recovery?" God knows what it is and has the way to get it to you. It is very helpful to have a relationship with God that is real and an ear to hear what the Spirit of God would say to you, so that your business can recover. By digging the ditches in faith, you provide an opportunity for God to fill them with solutions that have the ability to turn near disasters into current victories. As the opening scripture relates, God is as much God in the **hills** as He is also in the **valleys**. He doesn't want to be God only in the highs of our lives but wants to show us that He will also work in our valley experiences. Our valleys are more opportunities for Him to be God.

2. The Valley of Baca (Ps 84:5-6)

The Valley of Baca (weeping) is also overcome-able. Just as the psalmist wrote, you need to set your focus on a pilgrimage – a passing through where you are now. You make it a principle to never settle at the place of weeping or the place of despair. It may be alright to visit it a little bit, but you need to definitely move on and turn the weeping place into something else. Don't set up a base camp. In our Psalm, it was turned into a spring, so that pools of blessing become the new picture. Your motivation is not sorrow—don't replay the sad memories of the past and dwell on what could have been. Your motivation needs to be recovery and the desire to change what is currently in place to what it needs to be.

God is God in this valley as well. He made it a point to let the Syrians know that He was also God in the valleys and those who trust and push through the disappointments whilst relying on His strength in their predicaments, begin to see the capability of God in their least expected places. God will show you that the places of setbacks, disappointments, and weeping can be transformed into places of blessing, provision, and nourishment. How can He be God in our valley experiences unless He shows you He can?

The question we need to answer is this: "Will these extremities neutralize my faith and belief in God's capability, or will it motivate me to discover the help of a very present God in time of troubles?" **(Ps 46:1)**

3. The valley between Sochoh and Azekah (1 Sam 17:1)

A giant was present in this valley. Most of our valley experiences feel as if some gigantic opposition is standing in our way. Goliath stood up in the valley between Sochoh and Azekah and terrorized Israel, keeping them in retreat and being non-committal in their purpose for God. He succeeded in causing them to be intimidated with fear to the point where no one was going to do anything to change what they were facing. Goliath was just a bridge too far for them. Saul's entire army was paralyzed with fear, scrambling for whatever cover they could find. His size and booming presence kept Israel in **no man's land** for forty days and nights. No man's land was not breached. No one was progressing.

Where has your business been halted? Where has it ceased being effective? What giant is standing in your way? Are you beginning to feel intimidated by the lack of productivity in your marketplace?

The place they gathered at was a valley between Sochoh and Azekah known as *Ephes Dammim,* and is translated from the Hebrew to mean *a cessation of blood.* When two armies oppose each other, it is normally for the intention of a full-scale war where blood flow would be inevitable. But they were assembled prophetically at a place where a cessation of blood was prophesied. Blood would not flow, especially not Israel's. Goliath did not respect this. He did not realize that what he planned to do was already overshadowed by another outcome. In fact, the only blood that would eventually flow would be his. This Philistine had the gall to challenge the army of God. His size and skill was no match for the Lord of Hosts. David, even as teenager, understood this. He knew Goliath was an uncircumcised Philistine who had ventured onto ground that he could not handle. As big as he was, he was completely out of his depth.

Sometimes when we face giants in the marketplace we are tempted to run for cover because we know blood will flow, probably our own! But God makes the point clear that He is also God in our valleys. He is God in our valley of giants; in our valley of fear and intimidation; in our valley of hopeless causes.

Thankfully I can exercise my faith in the fact that my God is also able to be God in all my business lows. He definitely has a plan to rescue me. I don't have to expect myself to fail or to come in second again. I can have faith that things will turn because I can actually win this battle over my giant. **"...with God all things**

are possible." (**Matt 19:26**) This giant may be making a good point about my situation, and be able to muster a strong challenge against me, but he doesn't know that his warfare is futile. I am in covenant with God through Jesus's sacrifice on the cross. I have been called and anointed as a business king for Him. My destiny in the kingdom is a conduit of wealth flow. God is more than able to bring me up and out of where I am right now. There will not be a flow of blood where I am. God has primed me for recovery!

No matter what the struggle or the battle: GOD IS GOD IN ALL YOUR VALLEY CIRCUMSTANCES.

Chapter Twenty-Three

RISING UP FROM A PLACE OF DEATH

And he stretched himself out on the child three times, and cried out to the Lord and said, "O Lord my God, I pray, let this child's soul come back to him."

(1 Kings 17:21)

Jesus Christ is the same yesterday, today, and forever.

(Hebrews 13:8)

JESUS IS THE SAME YESTERDAY, TODAY, AND FOREVER

Elijah and Elisha demonstrated the power and synergy of a ministerial father and son working in the release of a double portion anointing. Elijah was asked by God to anoint Elisha as a prophet in his place, and from that day Elisha served him as a ministry son does his spiritual father. He waited on him, provided water for his hands, and was a constant companion, all the while learning from his character, lifestyle, and relationship with God.

As you observe the account of this relationship, of all the miracles that Elijah was used by God to accomplish, Elisha went on to produce double the bar set by Elijah.

And so it was, when they had crossed over, that Elijah said to Elisha, "Ask!

**What may I do for you, before I am taken
away from you?"
Elisha said, "Please let a double portion
of your spirit be upon me."**

(2 Kings 2:9)

The goal of any ministry son is to learn from his father and produce beyond what his father had been able to accomplish. This can be achieved because he sits under his father's anointing and catches what he has, adding that dimension to his own anointing and gifting from God when he is released. Hence, double!

We shouldn't be reinventing the wheel every time we do something. Are we not supposed to be moving **from generation to generation**, passing on to new generations what has been learned already? Both these prophets raised from the dead the sons of the women who had been kind to them and had made room for them in their lives. When you read the accounts of these raisings in **1 Kings 17:21** and **2 Kings 4:34**, it's fascinating to see how similar the experiences were. Elisha watched Elijah and worked from the platform he observed.

There is nothing new under the sun. Jesus has done it all before. He is the same today as He was back in Bible times. As sons of the Father, we should at least operate from the platform that Jesus said we could. He said that He did nothing unless He saw the Father doing it. Fathers need to raise sons in the ministry and turn their hearts to their sons, or else the earth will be visited with a curse. **(Malachi 4:6)** Fathers need to give their sons a picture of what can be accomplished in faith. It is this measure of faith that should be increasing in sons.

Businesses can recover. They have before, and because God never changes, they can now! God needs your business to live again and be brought back from the place of death that could be overshadowing it right now. Elijah prayed that the child's soul be returned to him so that he could live again. **(1 Kings 17:21)** When you lose your way in business, you often lose the soul of why you existed in the first place. Just as these women embraced the plan of God and the gift prophets sent to their vicinity by making room for them, God will help you recover and be productive once again. God knows how to revive the soul of our business purpose. You will need to embrace what He sends you. He will show you how to do things again. Be prepared to accept father figures—mentors with a financial anointing. These people have worked with God and have a testimony of what God is capable of. Find one that walks with a limp—it shows he has struggled with God and man and prevailed. **(Gen 32:25-31)** He has something to offer you more than a cheap quick fix. Become a son of a father or a son of a financial mentor so you can learn to prosper in double portion anointing. This will fulfill your call adequately.

RE-DIG THE WELLS

Elisha applied the methods used by Elijah and the results were the same. What works in business? What ensures leftovers, or cash flow? What keeps you protected? What comes back to you as profit? Revisit the **ancient paths** that others have followed for centuries and always had proven results. Practice financial integrity by doing what God says. **Re-lay** these concepts in your approach. **Revisit** these ancient paths. Imitate them and live. God is the same today as He always has been.

After Abraham dug wells in the desert and lived off their supply for years, the Philistines came and eventually stopped them up. Perhaps we should grasp this: THE WELLS MAY HAVE BEEN STOPPED UP, BUT THEY

STILL CONTAINED THE SAME WATER TO BRING LIFE TO ISAAC'S BASE THAT HAD KEPT ABRAHAM ALIVE. Isaac, the son, came and re-dug these wells and opened these ancient supply lines as they had been in his father's time. He even called them by their former names. **(Genesis 26:18-22)** We must embrace what our fathers have established. They are good starting points. But be prepared as you do for a surprise from God. God could cause you to discover **Rehoboth (v22)** your own, fresh, water supply. A well that is peculiar to you. Rehoboth means, **"For now the Lord has made room for us, and we shall be fruitful in the land."** Fathers lay the principles that lead us to our own anointing oil, that which defines our kingship.

To raise your business up from a place of death is not something that can't be done. We have basic models to follow and as we do, God will show what is right for 'you' to introduce further.

Chapter Twenty-Four

FOLLOW THE SIGNS

**"Thus speaks the Lord of hosts, saying:
'This people says, "The time has not
come, the time that the Lord's house
should be built.""'
Then the word of the Lord came by
Haggai the prophet, saying, "Is it time for
you yourselves to dwell in your paneled
houses, and this temple to lie in ruins?"**

(Haggai 1:2-4)

NOTHING TO SHOW FOR YOUR EFFORTS

One of the constant challenges a king-in-business faces is
the ability to balance between the time given to God and
that of running a business. Many financial kings initially
struggle with this scenario and often have an over-balance
on more time in the business and less God time or vice
versa.

The need to make budgets and targets is absolutely crucial
and the trap arranged by our enemy, is to distract us from
completing a healthy balance between the two. Mary and
Martha were hosting Jesus in **Luke 10:38-42**. Martha was
more concerned about the work of the house and what
needed to be done. Mary, **"...sat at Jesus' feet and heard
His word" (v39)** When Martha voiced her dissatisfaction,
Jesus said, **"Martha, Martha, you are worried and**

troubled about many things. But one thing is needed, and Mary has chosen that good part, which will not be taken away from her." (v41-42) Jesus showed us the importance of being in His presence. On the other hand, a business king cannot be only spiritually minded and neglect the practicalities of running a business successfully. There must be a balance between the time you give to God individually and the time required to concentrate on your business. This seems to be a common battle that kings-in-business encounter.

In the book of **Haggai,** God sent a **Prophet – Priest – King** synergy team to solve a serious problem that had crept into the lives of the people of Israel. The nation was working hard and diligently in everyday life, but had so little to show for it at the end of the day. We should all labour hard to show our commitment, diligence, and integrity, but must also be able to reveal the fruit of our labours.

Israel was provided with food and ate, but was never satisfied. There was always a need for more, no matter how much they brought home. They drank but could never be filled. Worse though, it seemed they worked hard at their employment and brought their money home to put it into purses that had holes in them. Their financial provisions just seemed to drain away unnaturally.

> **"You have sown much, and bring in little;**
> **You eat, but do not have enough;**
> **You drink, but you are not filled with drink;**
> **You clothe yourselves, but no one is warm;**
> **And he who earns wages,**
> **Earns wages to put into a bag with holes."**

> **(Haggai 1:6)**

> **"You looked for much, but
> indeed it came to little; and when you
> brought it home, I blew it away. Why?"
> says the Lord of hosts. "Because of My
> house that is in ruins, while every one of
> you runs to his own house.**
>
> (Haggai 1:9)

When this happens constantly we realize that something must be wrong. There is a pattern here; a sign that we should stop and investigate.

INSIGHTS INTO THEIR PREDICAMENT

The repair team was sent in to investigate and provide a solution for the people of Israel. Amongst their ranks was the **prophetic gift** with the word of God for the situation. The people had become over-balanced. They had fallen into the trap of spending more time developing and pursuing their own interests whilst the purposes of God were put on hold.

It seemed that Israel had slipped into looking after themselves only and allowing the physical presence of God (the outward appearance of their temple) to be neglected. They were building amazing homes and businesses for themselves and paying little attention to the house of God and its effect in the nation, and also the God who was responsible for their blessing. We are nothing without God. Everything we have has been given to us from Him. The business is not our resource—God is. He is the One who provides for us and sends us the clientele to be successful. It makes no sense to shut Him out while we pursue self-gain and comfort above His purpose.

Financial kings must be conscious of this trap. Our business does need constant attention, but it should never replace the value and intensity we need to place on our relationship with God. Becoming busy and building your business name and brand is so easy to do and can lead to the real issue of being put under pressure—remember Martha. Clearly God makes the point in Haggai that this needs to change, and quickly. The signs of getting it wrong are not hard to discover: all your labour bares very little financial fruit and stability. By drying up their financial comfort, God got Israel's attention. He was saying, "There is too much time being spent on your purposes and mine are left without much interest."

Your program is not more valuable than God's agenda and the place He needs to occupy in your life. You are a king-in-business to make money and be conduit of financial income into the church. That is your calling and ministry. God has a lost world to win and keep from going to hell. Your anointing has the power to create wealth **(Deut 8:18)** and it is this wealth that will help reach the lost in communities. The church must be active in winning the lost and being the hand of God where He is needed. Kings seriously help in advancing this purpose.

Whilst you enjoy the fruit of your labour, never neglect the purpose for which God has anointed you. Make sure you fulfill your part on the repair team. Your function will advance the kingdom of God significantly but it mustn't replace your personal love and desire for God. You must maintain the balance between building your paneled houses and making sure the place of God in your life (your personal relationship) and community are equally as important and given significant attention. In the New Testament we don't place or show our value of God through the state of the architecture of our buildings that represent our places of worship. Obviously there are people that look for this, but it isn't an indication of God's value. People are drawn to God today by the reality of His presence working in and through your life. You are the church today, not the buildings that people call church.

Sometimes recovery in business is as simple as sorting out the **right priorities** with the **right emphasis** on them. Am I giving the pursuit of wealth more passion and drive than my personal priesthood before God? Look at the fruit you are producing. Identify the signs.

Do you own a purse that has holes in it?

Chapter Twenty-Five

THE MANTLE-WRAPPING CONCEPT

So it was, when Elijah heard it, that he wrapped his face in his mantle and went out and stood in the entrance of the cave. Suddenly a voice came to him, and said, "What are you doing here, Elijah?"

(1 Kings 19:13)

THE WAY TO THE JUNIPER TREE

Elijah was a powerful, anointed, prophetic ministry in Israel. His prophetic anointing had established him as a person who knew God and who relayed what God was saying accurately. When he spoke a word to you from the Lord, that is exactly what it was—it was fulfilled in its season. **(Deut 18:21-22)**

After the great victory on Mt. Carmel where the false prophets and the Baal priests were killed, where the opinions of the people were dealt with, and a three and half year drought was broken through his word and prayer, Elijah received the word that Jezebel was after him and would not stop until he was dead. She wanted some revenge for what he had inflicted on her operation and quickly wanted to reinstate the false worship system. It seems ludicrous that this mighty gift, being used of God in an awesome display of power, would suddenly entertain fear and intimidation to the point that he fled for his life and arrived at a juniper tree in a serious state of depression.

> **But he himself went a day's journey into the wilderness, and came and sat down under a broom tree. And he prayed that he might die, and said, "It is enough! Now, Lord, take my life, for I am no better than my fathers!"**
>
> **(1 Kings 19:4)**

It was a difficult time for him. Perhaps he was reminded just how human he was and even though God had used him powerfully in the past, he now knew how vulnerable he could be outside of those times in the presence of God. When you feel that you have failed but your hopes were that at least you would go a little further than others have gone, is when this reality sets in. All Elijah's life's work and the miracles that God did through him meant nothing at that moment. He felt just as ordinary and vulnerable as the next person. Perhaps he realized how weak our frames were and how easy it was to fail in your flesh. He felt very weak and without purpose at that point and asked God to take him away. But God never leaves you nor forsakes you. When we are faithless, He remains faithful. **(2 Tim 2:13)**

Hagar also felt alone in the wilderness with no one actually knowing the extent of her pain, until God sent an angel to rescue her. She named the place; **Beer Lahai Roi**—*the God who lives and sees me.* **(Gen 16:13-14)** Just as God understood where she was emotionally and sent an angel to encourage her, God also sent an angel to rejuvenate Elijah and get him up on his feet again. He is the same yesterday, today, and forever. After great successes in the past, even if your current seasons have been extensively barren and prolonged, keep alive that God knows where you are and how to find you. He has a plan of recovery for you. He will remember you.

Elijah had allowed himself to inadvertently surrender to Jezebel's threats and found that he quickly went downhill into a state of depression and feelings of hopelessness. God's financial kings are not immune to this threat. This is not uncommon ground for kings-in-business. No matter how successful you may have been in previous years of trading, there is nothing more sobering and challenging than a prolonged season of quite to make you feel seriously wobbly and uncertain.

BURY YOURSELF IN YOUR MANTLE

Elijah finally completed the long journey to Mt. Horeb and went into a cave where during the night, when the word of the Lord came to him.

"What are you doing here, Elijah?"

(1 Kings 19:9)

It's almost as if God is asking, *why has this happened to you? This shouldn't be the outcome of your experience. You are a gift ministry and know My power and have seen it at work. How has this come about? What happened that this spirit of fear and intimidation was able to penetrate your heart and reduce you to these feelings?*

Perhaps like Peter did in the storm, when he walked on the water to Jesus, he suddenly realized when he saw the waves that people can't actually do this. It was at that point that he began to sink. The moment you feel that things are dependent on you, when you pit that to what God is actually doing by faith in your life and business call, that's when you start to melt in your humanity. When you remember how successful you have been as a king-in-business and now you can't seem to even spell *business*, is when you really feel and start to show your vulnerability. This is a good time to remember, **"You are of God, little children, and have overcome them, because He who is in you is greater than he who is in the world." (1 John 4:4)**

This is not what God planned for you. He will not leave you crumpled up on the side of the road under a broom tree. He wants you to recover and find the path again. It will require a visit to the **mountain of God** and a time to re-fire you and cause you to rediscover value and purpose. God will remind you of His strength and power but bring back to you the unmatched truths of the **"...still small voice"** and **the anointing in your mantle. (1 Kings 19:11-13)**

When Elijah saw the demonstrations of God's power from his cave and once again heard the whisper of God's voice within his spirit, **"...he wrapped his face in his mantle and went out and stood in the entrance of the cave." (1 Kings 19:13)** For me this underlines the road to your recovery. It is not a matter of a power display on the outside, but rather the ability to hear what God is saying in the midst of the battle you are going through. Once you can hear that again and you wrap yourself in your kingly business mantle, it will lead to a return of a power manifestation in your business. Success will miraculously reappear because you have heard the **"...still small voice" (v12)** to your current situation, and picked up **the mantle of your purpose,** wrapping yourself **into** it. You rediscover the power and value of the anointing God has put on you. We all have a gift anointing from God—a mantle that separates us from others. We all have **a rod of God** in our hands that is designed to perform the miracles our lives and purposes require. **(Exod 4:2-17)** This is the secret. This is what dejected kings-in-business need to do rediscover. Time out at God's mountain place is crucial for you to reconnect with spiritual power, anointing and purpose.

Your recovery is imminent. Quiet the threatening voices of your Jezebel and take timeout at God's mountain retreat. Rest in His presence. Eat food prepared by angels. Water yourself on the Spirit of God and feed on His faithfulness. Don't look for the power manifestations before you rediscover the sensitivity to hear the whisper of the Spirit to you. Then believe in the anointing God has clothed you with and wrap yourself in that stance. God will soon redirect your purpose.

You will once again know what it feels like to recover without fail.

Chapter Twenty-Six

FAITH FOR DESPERATE TIMES

And she went up and laid him on the bed of the man of God, shut the door upon him, and went out. Then she called to her husband, and said, "Please send me one of the young men and one of the donkeys, that I may run to the man of God and come back."
So he said, "Why are you going to him today? It is neither the New Moon nor the Sabbath."
And she said, "It is well."

(2 Kings 4:21-23)

GOD'S PROMISES WON'T FAIL IN OUR CIRCUMSTANCES

This woman in our story had taken care of Elisha and looked after his needs when on his journey around the country, sharing the Word of God. She had recognized the call and gifting on Elisha and gone out of her way to honour this ministry gift sent from God. The Bible refers to her as a *noble woman*.

On one of the visits, Elisha wanted to show his gratitude for the care he had received frequently from her and her family. He wanted to bless her in some way.

And he said to him, "Say now to her, 'Look, you have been concerned for us with all this care. What can I do for you? Do you want me to speak on your behalf to the king or to the commander of the army?' "
She answered, "I dwell among my own people."
So he said, "What then is to be done for her?"
And Gehazi answered, "Actually, she has no son, and her husband is old."

(2 Kings 4:13-14)

To be able to continue the family line was of real significance in Israel. Having a son to pass on an inheritance was important. Obviously this family had problems in this area and I am sure that after much heartache, had resigned themselves to accept that this was not going to happen for them. That is why she probably answered in the manner she did when Elisha told her that she would have a child within a year's time. She was moved with emotion because of all previous failings and said, **"No, my lord. Man of God, do not lie to your maidservant!" (v16)**

She had probably laid this desire to have an heir in her life down and to be suddenly told that what she had wanted for so long would now become a reality was extremely hard to entertain. She didn't want to suffer any disappointments.

This was a different situation. This promise came unexpectedly from quarters not normal to man. It came from a prophet of God with the Word of the Lord on his lips. It came from the throne room of God. This son was a

218

promise from God and to authenticate Elisha's word, he was born at the time that was spoken.

True to form though, the enemy stepped in and played his hand. Where God wants to heal, restore, and further you in abundance, the enemy comes to destroy, distract, kill, and maim. One day this little boy—the miracle heir—dies. The potential of the fulfilled promises from God—the possibility of a heritage—suddenly lay lifeless in the woman's hands. What a shock to her system! This was the last thing this family needed. After all the previous years of disappointments and then to have a son at last, only to have him taken away so unexpectedly, was really a bridge too far. Do God's promises die? Do they fade on you? How she reacted to this tragedy would be crucial to the final outcome.

FAITH REACTIONS

Many people in the Bible reached these desperate times. David for example was going to be stoned by his mighty men for the hurt that suddenly came on them. **(1 Samuel 30)** Had they followed through with their emotions, they would have missed God's recovery plan. In that desperate moment, David needed an outcome that would lead to success and eventual victory. He had to find the silver lining in the darkest clouds imaginable. He did, and so can we. **(1 Sam 30:6-8)**

The widow of Zarepath **(1 Kings 17:13-15)** also faced a life and death situation. Her circumstances were so severe that she and her son were about to die from starvation, caused by a famine, ravaging the land at that time. That is when she bumped into Elijah who had a word from God for her. Her response would determine her outcome. God painted a picture for her through the prophetic words given by Elijah. God does the same for us week in and week out.

We sit under the ministry of the word of God and these pictures are created for us. The widow accepted what God was showing her and she responded in faith. She lived to tell the story. Kings must position themselves to hear the rhema (now) words of God that lead to recovery.

Simeon for example, received a proceeding word—a promise that he would not see death until he saw the consolation of Israel. **(Luke 2:25-27)** From the time he was given this promise until it was fulfilled, not even death could come near him. God upholds what comes from Him.

Our Shunammite woman was just as desperate. The promised son arrived when he was supposed to because God fulfilled not only His promise but the timing as well. The little lad was out in the fields with his father one day when he felt ill and suddenly died so unexpectedly. His mother sprang into a faith reaction that was simply amazing. She insisted that THIS COULD NOT BE. **"God is not a man, that He should lie…." (Num 23:19)** He would not promise something and then not allow it to be fulfilled. Jesus is **"…the author and finisher of our faith…" (Heb 12:2)** Whatever He says will reach the purpose it was given.

The Shunammite woman held onto the promises of God that came from this gift ministry sent to her. She believed her man of God. She believed the prophetic word spoken to her. She kept her emotions in check, which considering the situation, was extremely challenging, and took the child back to the source of the promise. This distraction, though serious, was not going to rule the day. In like manner, Jesus was on his way to raise Jairus's daughter from a sick bed at one point in His ministry. Just before He reached his house they received word that she was dead. Here was the distraction. Jesus told him, **"Do not be afraid; only believe." (Mark 5:36)** This is the faith the Shunammite displayed. Elisha was away, and so she placed her son on Elisha's bed (the source of the promise) and went in search for him. Along the way, she would say when asked, *all is well*. Her whole demeanor spelled out that what has occurred was not going to be permanent. Things as they were now would change. When she eventually found Elisha the first thing she says was:

> **"Did I ask a son of my lord? Did I not say, 'Do not deceive me'?"**
>
> **(2 Kings 4:28)**

She had not asked for this blessing. It was freely given by permission of God and intended to bless and fulfill all that she had originally wanted. She was not going to be robbed out her destiny. She went straight back to the source of her promise and put God in remembrance of His word. She had an end picture in mind and was not allowing anything to derail it. Her son was raised back to life.

Sometimes recovery requires resilience on our part—a resilience that says, *thus far and no further*. Things will change to where they are supposed to be. *This is what God said* and therefore our circumstances will change. He does not promise what He can't deliver. It requires that you go back to your source and hold on to what you have been told. Don't give up without a fight of faith. Remember the Shunammite woman insisting that *all is well*. He alone knows how to raise our hope and keep His promises alive that have become threatened.

God has recovery in mind for you where the devil has tried to stop up your well!

Chapter Twenty-Seven

RECOVERY OF PERSONAL FINANCES

**And Adam knew his wife again, and she
bore a son and named him Seth, "For
God has appointed another seed for me
instead of Abel, whom Cain killed."**
(Genesis 4:25)

FINANCIAL OBEDIENCE

When it comes to personal finances, God has recovery as
well as an economic plan in place to help establish and
prosper every believer. Your response to His strategy will
help you in today's unsteady and uncertain marketplace
environments. God can and will do anything. No matter
where you are on the economic ladder of success and
financial stability, working with God's principles will
always advance you further. God didn't qualify the
economic level of people, race, or geographic location that
He would assist. He simply said to see, **"...If I will not
open for you the windows of heaven..."** (Mal 3:10). No
matter where you are financially, God will honour your
obedience and trust. The amount does not disqualify you or
nullify the principles of the Word of God from working on
your behalf. The point is to determine whether you trust
God enough to be obedient financially.

I once heard that as little as 12% of the known church
worldwide tithed. If this is accurate then there is a huge
population of churchgoers that don't benefit from God's

plan to protect and provide for His people, especially when God asks us to test Him in tithing to see whether He will open heaven's windows for us. There is no need for people to struggle or just cope economically. It's just not necessary to live and exist on the bare minimum when God gives us a way to avoid it. Whatever the reasons, it is not for me to judge the actions of others. It just seems that what God wants to do for them financially is at a perpetual loss, should they persist in their current thinking.

God is quite serious about money. He is just and fair and is also known in a covenantal manner, as *the Lord our compensation (Jehovah Gmolah)*. God wasn't going to allow the Egyptians to live off of 430 years of free labour from Israel without compensation. God ordered that Israel plunder the Egyptians when they left and take gold, silver, and clothing from their captors. **(Exod 12:35-36)**

Also, He challenged the priests of Israel in **Malachi 1** for allowing the people to bring sub-standard offerings (physically deformed sacrifices such as one-eyed calves or three-legged sheep) that caused the value and respect God required, to wane abysmally. This was a direct violation of what the priests were supposed to uphold and because of this the people ended up suffering financially. The priests were demonstrating by their non-correction of this practice, that God was not really worth the effort and any old giving would be fine. WRONG!

In the book of **Haggai 1**, God sends a prophet to tell the people that the lack of provision in the nation was due to them building their personal comfort as precedence over building the image of God in the nation. They had said that it was not time to build the temple **(vs2-4)**, and so God acted to gain their attention. He blew away what they brought home, **"Because of My house that is in ruins,**

while every one of you runs to his own house." (Haggai 1:9)

I wonder if many people struggle today in the church for similar reasons? I wonder if today's priests find it too controversial to talk about finances as they should? I wonder if they allow substandard giving disorders in the church today? I wonder if they realize how serious this is to God? If they don't, it will nullify their understanding of the value of giving to God as an essential principle in the supply of their own personal provision. What are your financial indicators suggesting? Is God trying to get your attention? What signs are following your understanding of God's economic policies?

The facts are simple. God wants you to have enough to live on, and enough to be a blessing to others in need while being able to sow into your local church and the kingdom. He has implemented a financial strategy that will suit all who will trust and believe. God can and does accelerate your financial position when you submit to His principles willingly.

ACCELERATION THROUGH SUPERNATURAL PROVISION

Acceleration is the dream of every business king. They want their businesses to succeed and be constantly fruitful and achieve what they set out to do in their planning stages. They look to accelerate more, especially where they have been pressurized by lack over an extended period of time. Business becomes very hard when cash flow is a problem.

The point of this section is to show you that God does accelerate your business and personal finances. He does break through the breach like water. **(2 Sam 5:20)** There are times when he supernaturally boosts your finances, and the increase—like a flood—places you at a completely different place from where you were. It is not wrong to believe God will do this because He has already demonstrated His willingness to do so several times in the Word. To expect this type of supernatural acceleration every time could lead to disappointment.

Many business kings become disappointed when they feel let down because the acceleration they needed didn't come as they thought. God does accelerate supernaturally—there is no doubt about it—but keep it in perspective. How many people do you know who have gone down to the sea and pulled out a fish with the supply of their own personal tax in its mouth? But God showed in His Word that Peter was told to do that, and he did. That's why it is called supernatural acceleration.

Let's recall some examples of where God has accelerated people and their financial situations:

1. The widow and her son (1 Kings 17:8-24)

The first picture we see of this particular widow is one where she is out collecting wood to make a fire, so she and her son could eat their last meal, before starvation from a severe famine would end their lives. The duration of the famine had completely depleted her resources. They were both in a critical position and in need of a recovery plan if there was to be one.

Elijah came right into her desperate situation. It's almost like the story of Zacchaeus who climbed a tree just to get a glimpse of Jesus, but Jesus instead walked to the tree Zacchaeus was in and spoke to him. (**Luke 19:1-10**) Likewise, God brought His answer right to where our widow was in desperation and anguish. He arrived with a plan of recovery, but it was based on a spiritual principle.

When God brings an answer to your situation, it may come from a human (as it was in this case), and therefore you could be challenged whether you want to believe it. If you don't honour the gift you won't receive the reward. **(Matt 10:41)** Believing that a person has God's answer for a situation is not new in biblical history. God has always battled to get His people to believe Him and the gift ministries He sends. There are examples where believing the people sent did occur but they are outweighed by those who didn't. The Thessalonians were complimented by Paul for their ability to receive what God was saying, even though a man delivered the message. **(1 Thess 2:13)** The writer of the book of Hebrews also pointed out the necessity of accepting the word as coming from God and to mix it with faith if we are to profit from it. **(Heb 4:2)**

Elijah's word may have been spiritual in origin but nevertheless would require a natural outworking if it were to change their current situation. A gift ministry with a spiritual principle to establish the widow's recovery visited her. She had to accept that Elijah had the answer for her circumstance and that God had sent him. Only when she obeyed did she step into the recovery plan that totally accelerated her situation.

We are no different than this widow. We also are presented with opportunities that can take us out of where we are, but must make the choice to obey. What Elijah said to her was personally quite challenging. It could have been perceived as a self-gain project for meeting his own needs. Sadly there is plenty of this evidence and abuse in the church today that has resulted in many business kings not trusting what God could to do financially in their circumstances.

Elijah did present a principle that resulted in a harvest because that is what the circumstance required: **Give to God first—give to the man of God representing the presence of God, first.** She obeyed the principle and lived to tell the story. The power of the famine and its horrendous consequences rampaging in her life were broken at that moment. God supernaturally accelerated her situation from a definite death outcome, to one of life and ongoing life. It might have taken a little while for her supplies to finally run out when the famine began, and for her to be in desperate need, but when she met Elijah and heard God's word, it took her trust and obedience to release her **immediate** recovery plan from God.

There is such an important concept for God's priests (those who lead congregations) in this story. Emotionally one would ask, *Who could ask a poor, about-to-die family to give what little they have, FIRST, to a man of God in their midst, or to the church in some way?* It could easily have been misconstrued that because Elijah was in the same predicament, and he was just out to take care of himself. Most leaders won't ask such a thing because of the emotional implications attached to it. Religion and religious mindsets and the frequent abuse by people in authority have forced many leaders to stay away from this approach. Just because it may have been abused in the past, does not mean it is not a biblical principle of financial recovery. Had Elijah not spoken or challenged the way he did, the family would have perished. No doubt about it. This was God's answer for her recovery. Despite her situation she still had to follow the principle of honouring God first; to honour the man of God in your midst—to honour the gift ministry sent to help you. Emotions don't save you—obedience to God's rhema words do!

Your circumstances should not be allowed to dictate how you respond to God. These principles are not subject to our natural economy and have worked endlessly throughout time. They should never stop you from honouring and doing what is right with God. They simply don't fail at any time. Knowing how to appropriate them timeously may be a challenge, but God's word cannot return to Him void. Christians shouldn't stop tithing or giving simply because their situations have become financially challenging. This is the time when believers need to particularly show their trust and commitment to the principles that govern God's financial package. How do you show they work and become a testimony to others, if they don't work in tough economic seasons? Lean times can especially be used to prove the validity that God's financial principles work, regardless.

This widow trusted that even though she saw no way out of where she was God obviously had one. As a result, her acceleration was amazing. God accelerated her from a death-defining situation to one of life. How can you measure that in terms of currency?

2. The widow's jar of oil (2 Kings 4:1-7)

This particular widow (a different one than in the previous story) was on the brink of losing her sons to the creditors as payment for her dead husband's business debts. **(v1)** You can sense the urgency in her cry when she addresses Elisha. So many business kings have cried out to God in urgency and desperation. Mercifully God is touched with the feelings of our infirmities. He cares about us all and those who know how to turn to Him find that He is a very present help in time of trouble. **(Ps 46:1)** God doesn't skirt around the problem. When Moses was concerned about the people asking who had sent him to help the captives in Egypt with a recovery plan from God, God said to tell them that *I AM* sent him. **(Exod 3:14)** Not *I Was* or *I Am Going to Be*, but *I AM* what you may require in every situation, is going to assist you. Whatever the present situation would turn out to be, *I AM* would be equal to it.

God had a recovery plan for our widow as well and again it involved obedience to the word of a prophet, a gift ministry that God had connected to her. God's recovery plan was aimed at accelerating her finances dramatically so she not only paid her husband's debts and kept her sons to build the family heritage, but it also involved a pension scheme that would provide for her for the rest of her life. God does not think the way we do. His thoughts are not our thoughts. **(Isa 55:8)** We are trained to accept that *just enough* is healthy and politically correct in the church. The widow experienced drastic acceleration; she went from having very little to a place where she would have enough to live on for the rest of her life. We must take thoughtful note of this next point: her level of acceleration was an amazing boost to her financial position, but it depended on how seriously she took the word to gather empty vessels—and not only a few **(v3)**. *Just enough* wouldn't have worked. She had to gather *more than enough*. The onus was completely on her. She determined the acceleration she received by her response to the word from the prophet. She even decided the cut-off point.

> **Now it came to pass, when the vessels were full, that she said to her son, "Bring me another vessel."**

And he said to her, "There is not another vessel." So the oil ceased.

(2 Kings 4:6)

Somehow this concept seems to be important with God. When Pharaoh was asked when he wanted the plague of frogs to be removed from Egypt, he replied, "tomorrow." **(Exod 8:10)** From that time on God waited until the next day before He removed some of the other plagues. **(Exod 8:29; 9:5-18; and 10:4)**

Many times in business, we determine our own outcome. We drive that bus. The onus is on us to hear God and go for the result that is needed. God wants us to have abundantly and not stop short of that mark. God always had leftovers, even if it was for the feeding of thousands of people at one time. We learn that *more than enough* is acceptable. Don't go for less because it may feel religiously polite. Don't be afraid to trust God for acceleration beyond what is usual for you.

3. Naomi's life and purpose (Ruth 4:4-17)

Naomi and Elimelech left their hometown of Bethlehem for the land of Moab. The meaning of *Bethlehem* is translated to be *a house of bread*, where there was stability and the provision required to live. This husband and wife team decided to move to Moab, meaning *the seed of the father*. Moab was the son of Lot and was conceived and born out of an incestuous relationship through the actions of Lot's daughters. Why would you move from a place of provision and stability to a land rooted in a spirit of lust and incest?

Upon the move, all things went wrong for them. Naomi lost her husband and her two sons. When she returned to Bethlehem she asked not be called *Naomi* (meaning

231

pleasant), but rather *Marah* (*bitter*). She came back to her hometown a broken and hurt woman without the means to support herself. Naomi needed a recovery plan from God.

The least likely asset she had at that stage was Ruth, her daughter-in-law. Ruth had decided to stay and support her even though it would be a great sacrifice to her personally. But God used Ruth to accelerate a recovery, not only for herself, but for Naomi as well. Through Ruth's marriage to Boaz, God boosted Naomi's recovery amazingly:

a. Ruth was the source of Naomi getting her land back. **(Ruth 4:5-6)**

b. Naomi got to nurse a grandchild when this was seemingly impossible at one stage. **(Ruth 4:16)**

c. Naomi had prophetic words of gaining, **"a restorer of life and a nourisher of your old age." (Ruth 4:15)**

d. Naomi played a role in nursing Ruth's son, Obed. He was the grandfather of King David, a most powerful king in all Israel and a man after God's own heart. **(Ruth 4:17)** She had a hand in shaping one of Israel's greatest kings of all time.

e. She recovered to the level as if she had seven sons born to her. **(Ruth 4:15)**

Although Naomi came home with no real future, the least asset she thought she had turned out to be the catalyst God used to change not only her, but also Ruth's. You can't measure this acceleration in money terms, but both their lives were accelerated to a level they could not have foreseen. God can do the same for your business and accelerate it to a level unimagined.

4. Joseph—from prison to prime minister (Gen 41:40-44)

Joseph's life was on a high when he was young and living under his father's roof. He had the coat of many colours (meaning he was the favoured son), and in addition had the blessing of God to receive directional dreams with their accurate interpretations. One dream depicted he would be in a place of power and authority with others bowing down to him, his brothers included. However, the jealousy Joseph's brothers developed toward him caused this gift-wrapped life to come under pressure and seemingly spiral out of control. They wanted to get rid of him and waited for an opportunity to present itself. When it did, Joseph went from being thrown into a pit, to being sold to traders bound for Egypt, where he was eventually sold in a slave market to become a servant in Potiphar's house. Finally, he was falsely accused and sent to the king's prison where the key was thrown away for these types of dangerous inmates.

This valley in his life's timeline lasted approximately thirteen years—a long time to feel that you have been forgotten and your purpose in life had passed its sell-by-date plan. But then in one day, God accelerated him from a man with no hope, a man hidden away from society and serving a jail term for life, to the prime minister of all Egypt, where only Pharaoh was senior to him in rank. Joseph was positioned for his destiny in only one day. That is what I call acceleration.

It matters not what precedes your transformation, even if it is a long and difficult time. It will be a training ground for what God has purposed in your future. Your recovery plan from God may or may not involve a similar boost of this magnitude, but either way you can believe God to change what is currently keeping you from your destiny. When it's time to accelerate into the next phase of your development as a person or business king for God, nothing will be able to stop it. When God starts the repositioning, it happens quickly.

How will your business regain ground? How will you get to a place of acceleration in business terms? Our previous examples show that it came by obedience to a gift ministry sent to you. In this example, all Joseph had was the promise of the proceeding word God had spoken earlier in his life. It would be fulfilled. What are your proceeding words from God? Put God in remembrance of them and keep going in faith. God is not a man that He should lie. **(Num 23:19)** What He has promised He will fulfill. Build yourself up by releasing these declarations as a given fact. Then make sure that your business plan is practical and sound and that it has the infrastructure to work in the marketplace. It's no good having your head in the clouds and your feet stumbling on the ground. God knows how to change the wind's direction and rain in new deals and clients meant to be on your turf anyway.

ACCELERATION BY CHOOSING TO OBEY THE WORD

The biggest challenge in the believer's life comes in two simple folders:

1) Obedience
2) Acceptance

The Bible talks about the fruit of obedience in very positive and colourful ways. It is a trait that always results in blessing. God tells us that obedience is also better than sacrifice. **(1 Sam 15:22)** You will hear very exciting things about God, His word, and what He can do; but until you obey, you won't collide with what it has to offer.

The Word of God is not just for reading. We need to put into practice the now words that God speaks to us. God brings these rhema words to us personally **(Matt 4:4)** or through others He sends to us. We have to know how to discern them. That's why acceptance is crucially important. Accepting the word spoken by a man or woman of the faith as a word from God, is a major mindset challenge. As I mentioned earlier, Paul commended the Thessalonian church for winning this battle. They accepted the words spoken by men, as those spoken by God to them. **(1 Thess 2:13)** Countless thousands of believers sit in churches on Sundays all around the world and many remain unchanged because they waver between opinions—is this God or man?

This is the battle Elijah had with the people of God on Mount Carmel. **(1 Kings 18:21)** The word has to be mixed with faith before it can profit you. **(Heb 4:2)** There are checks and balances you can apply. But once you believe that what was spoken is God's word to you, you should show your acceptance by the application you release. Isaiah teaches that the word of God will profit you, **(Isa 48:17-18)** but you must first of all accept it as God's word to your heart. The word profiting you is also tied up in keeping His way, which will ultimately lead you to **"inherit the land."** **(Ps 37:34)** To keep God's way, you have to believe, remember, and accept what God is saying and show faith by applying the word to your situation.

There is a classic example of this principle found in Israel's history. The people of Ephraim turned back in the face of battle, even though they were adequately armed and well able to overcome their opposition. There are three reasons cited for this and one of them was that **"They refused to**

walk in His law." (Ps 78:9-11) When you hear and believe the now words of God to you, and walk with them, it shows your acceptance. That's when you enjoy the breakthroughs God has for you. Remember that we make our way prosperous and enjoy good success by the application we show to the word of God. **(Josh 1:8)** There definitely is scope for breakthrough in relation to your performance in believing and accepting the word to yourself.

THE BIG FIVE IN FINANCIAL RECOVERY

When it comes to personally accelerating financially, it is imperative that we familiarize ourselves with God's financial packages. In my working with Christian business people and running churches for many years, as well as travelling extensively, I have discovered that numerous church members have knowledge of these packages in a bits and pieces measure. These packages are designed to succeed in our economic systems and therefore warrant at least a full investigation and understanding. Having some knowledge of one principle and some more of another will not be sufficient to create enough of a stable environment to change your financial situation.

I live in South Africa and one of the major draw cards for tourism in our nation is our game reserves. We have what we call the **"The Big Five"** in African wildlife and even have our currency printed with pictures of these animals. The Big Five include: elephant, buffalo, rhinoceros, lion, and leopard. People come from all over the world to see our Big Five in their natural habitat.

I believe when it comes to accelerating or recovering personally in your finances, God has **The Big Five** in scripture. Again this is something you choose to implement, and those who have, often testify that they experienced an immediate acceleration in their financial

236

circumstances. Not only that but they become amazed at how God supernaturally provided for them by causing their money to stretch and last through the month, where on paper it looked like an accounting impossibility. But with God, there is always a completely different outcome. Obedience to these principles causes God's miraculous to be evident. This is what most people need. It is not just the monthly provisions that highlight the miraculous ways God comes through for you that must be taken into account. When you look back over your life after being consistently faithful and obedient to these principles for years, you can literally measure the goodness of God's care toward you— how He has gone before you and provided for you in ways unimaginable. It is so blatantly obvious.

What is neat about these principles is that they are relative to where you are and to your personal situation. Anyone— regardless of race, colour, and experiences—can benefit. Where you are personally on the economic success ladder is not the point. When understanding comes and you apply the principles faithfully, you will move upwards towards stability and increase that is relative to you. But you can increase beyond this as well. The onus is on you.

What we must also understand about God's financial package is that wrapped up in His Big Five are certain fruits that accompany them. These fruits are a real blessing and must become a motivation in us. We should make it our practice to look for and expect these fruits to be present when we deal obediently with our response to God's financial package. There are obviously many references to finance in the Bible, but these five consistently sum up the main approach to understanding God's financial package. God's **Big Five** include:

1) Tithing **(Mal 3:8-10) (Gen 4:4) (Gen 14:20)**
2) Giving **(Mal 3:8) (Luke 6:38)**

3) Sowing **(Gen 26:1-3) (Gen 26:12-16)**
4) First Fruits **(Gen 4:4) (Rom 11:16)**
5) Alms Giving **(Prov 19:17) (Ps 41:1-2)**

As already stated, many Christians have some knowledge of these principles but it would definitely benefit to have more understanding of how they work. **Knowledge** without **understanding** cannot produce **wisdom**.

THE FIVE FRUITFUL "P's" IN GOD'S FINANCIAL PACKAGE

Each principle is a **key** to breakthrough in a particular area, but only the right keys work in the right locks. Let's take a brief look at The Big Five financial principles and the fruit they produce should we choose to obey:

1. **Tithing releases the fruit of PROTECTION (Mal 3:8-12)**

One of the biggest misunderstandings that people have in regard to tithing for example, is now that they have tithed, they have given to God and they expect it will be given back to them. **(Luke 6:38)** They are correct to expect a return, except that tithing is the wrong key to open the lock of provision. You never give a tithe. It belongs to God anyway. **(Lev 27:30)** It belonged to God even before the law was present. **Abel** and **Abraham** show us this concept clearly. Before tithing became a principle in Jewish law, there were people already practicing it. Rather than giving, you **bring** your tithe to your storehouse so that there may be food in God's house. It is not given. It shows God that you honour the gift ministry in your storehouse and you believe the word of God. It also lets God know that

238

money does not have control over you, but that He has your heart. Money is a true measure of the heart condition when it comes to where God is on your agenda. Do we run after God, or do we love money more? That is why the book of Malachi talks about the nation robbing God. The Priests action at that time allowed the people to lose their focus on the value God placed on Tithing. **(Mal 1)**

Tithing is crucial to your survival. It opens the window of heaven above your circumstances **(Mal 3:10)** because of your willingness to bring to God what belongs to Him. But it is not solely responsible for what comes through heaven's window into your life. That is why we must understand the fruit that each key unlocks. If you continue reading this chapter in **Malachi** you will see that tithing produces the fruit of **protection**:

    a.   I will rebuke the devourer for your sakes **(Mal 3:11)**
    b.   Your fruit will not be destroyed on the ground **(v11)**
    c.   Your vine will not fail to produce in the field **(v11)**
    d.   Spoken by the **Lord of Hosts (v11)**

It continues in **verse 12** to say that nations will call you blessed and you will be a delightful land. The mention of the *The Lord of Hosts* is also significant. There are several references in the Bible where *The Lord of Hosts* appears to do battle on behalf of the purposes of God, underlining the fact that God will protect what has been called on. If there is one thing a family or business needs in today's financial world, it is the fruit of protection where what is supposed to be produced, materializes. The markets are so unstable and uncertain that people can lose almost everything if they collapse, but God promises protection when you are a tither.

When individuals and businesses tithe they open themselves up to the protection God promises to afford them respectively.

It makes perfect sense for companies and businesses to include a place for God's tithe in their budgeting. This way you guarantee God's protection for your obedience. The devourer is not allowed to cross these lines. God says He will rebuke him. Added to this protection are the promises that your fruit will not be destroyed on the ground, nor the production of fruit be impeded. **(Mal 3:11)** In this way, your family and businesses can enjoy the goodness of God should economies collapse and markets crash. God's system of economics is not subject to the world's. **Tithing** is the **key** that produces this fruit. Not giving. You don't give to have the fruit of protection. You have to use the right key in the right lock to open the right provision. I believe many people in the body of Christ are not fully aware of the fundamental keys that unlock the secrets of supernatural provision. Instead, people become frustrated because what is supposed to work (according to their understanding), doesn't. We must then consider which key we are using to open the door we require.

2. Giving releases the fruit of PROVISION (Luke 6:38)

Giving is the key that creates provision for you. The measure you use is the same measure God will use with you. So if you give sparingly, you will reap the same.

It seems to me that tithing opens the windows of heaven in readiness for the blessing God wants to pour out. But your measure of giving determines the amount coming back to you. The onus and responsibility is completely up to you. So when there is lack on the horizon, giving is a key that changes that situation. Jesus said that it was more blessed to give than receive **(Acts 20:35)**. Being a giver ensures constant supernatural returns from the hand of God. You can never out give God.

3. Sowing releases the fruit of PROSPERITY (Gen 26:12-16)

Sowing is the key that brings you prosperity. You sow to get a harvest. Farmers sow seed to attain a certain crop. Harvests are always abundant in their returns. You will prosper from a good harvest. There are some rules we should know about sowing:

a. You always sow into good soil.
b. You never sow out of compulsion.
c. You sow in kind to reap what you need.
d. You sow willingly and freely.
e. You sow where God tells you, regardless of what it looks like.

Isaac sowed in a famine **(Gen 26:1-3)**. No farmer would waste his seed sowing where he knows there will be no return. Isaac sowed in obedience to God. He sowed because God told him to and reaped that same year a hundredfold blessing. **(Gen 26:12)** He prospered, and as you read further, God continued to prosper him until he became very prosperous. **(v13)** Any person or business owner that reaps a hundred fold in one year would consider himself to be truly blessed. This is the potential that the concept of sowing carries. Sowing in obedience and sowing into good soil will result in a prosperous harvest. Look at the following scriptures to compound your understanding:

a. Whilst the earth remains there will always be a seedtime and a harvest. A sower will always have a return. **(Gen 8:22)**

b. When you sow to enhance or increase something, the measure you use will be what God uses to bring a return to you. **(Prov 11:24-25)**

c. You need to realize that God will bless your sowing. Do not try and work out when and how. **(Eccles 11:6)**

d. God will always make sure that a sower will have seed to sow, therefore guaranteeing a return. **(2 Cor 9:10)**

4. **First Fruits release the fruit of PERMEATION (Rom 11:16)**

The giving of first fruits leads to the fruit of permeation. It involves the giving of your *first* to God. God accepted Abel's sacrifice and not Cain's because Abel gave the **fat** of his **first** to God. **(Gen 4:4)** God puts a high regard on those who practice this concept. When you examine the book of Proverbs you will discover that the honouring of first fruits always lead to plenty and overflowing vats (excess).

Businesses must have excess or they cannot be a blessing to God's kingdom purpose. They are not meant to just exist and cover costs. But the abundance referred to is preceded by **"Honor the Lord with your possessions, And with the first fruits of all your increase; So your barns will be filled with plenty, And your vats will overflow with new wine." (Prov 3:9-10)** God promises that the giving of our first from all our increases will result in this form of fullness and overflow. Paul spoke about first fruits and the effect it had on the whole loaf. **(Rom 11:16)** The giving of the first fruit permeates through the whole batch making the remaining 90% just as holy as the first 10%. God will bless the balance as much as He does the initial first fruit amount. It is this first portion that carries the blessing to the whole batch.

5. **Alms Giving releases the fruit of PRESERVATION (Ps 41:1-2)**

The fruit of alms giving is preservation. Notice that this portion of scripture says, **"Blessed is he who considers the poor; The Lord will deliver him in time of trouble. The Lord will preserve him and keep him alive, And he will be blessed on the earth; You will not deliver him to the will of his enemies."** It goes on to mention that even on his sick bed he will be strengthened and sustained.

When you willingly provide for those who can't provide for themselves, God promises to preserve you not only in financial trouble but also on your sick bed. The way for a business to beat tough economic times is to be preserved by God and that also comes as a result of the way you have kept others alive in their tough seasons. Include in your budget planning the preservation of the poor in some way, and God will make sure you are preserved in your tough times. Find the poor in your community and bless them or assist with their recovery and understand that you have now insured yourself against a similar fate when economic trouble does come.

THE MEASURE OF MERCY

Remember the measure you use will be how God will return blessing to you. For me it seems that what touches the heart of God is when those who are in a place of ascendency or authority, show mercy willingly to those who can't help themselves. That's how we are with God. He showed us mercy when we couldn't help ourselves. When we were dead in our trespasses and sins, He sent Jesus to die for us. We couldn't pay the price that was required. So when businesses exercise mercy from their place of strength towards those who can't help themselves, God is drawn to that.

Believers should spend some time rethinking the make-up and merits of God's financial package. It has been established to accelerate personal stability despite the state of national or world economies. The secret is to be aware of what key opens which door. As you faithfully abide in the understanding and faith expectations of what the various keys produce, so you will be rewarded by the One who created these keys for your benefit. Recovery is not a problem to God. It is a matter of when you want to begin!

ACCELERATION THROUGH LIFESTYLE

When thinking of acceleration in personal finances don't just think of supernatural amounts coming to you, although this does happen and there are ways to create these opportunities; nor should you think that it can only happen as you obey certain principles. This is also the case but we need to take cognizance of all of God's financial keys and obey them in the right environments. There will be an immediate result. We also accelerate when we realize that the lifestyle and way we conduct our lives will also generate financial opportunities. The Psalmist wrote:

**"Whoever offers praise glorifies Me;
And to him who orders his conduct aright
I will show the salvation of God."**

(Ps 50:23)

Those who order their conduct according to what is right with God will see the salvation God can produce. Just a hint of what God's salvation can produce in life is also recorded in the book of Psalms:

**Blessed be the Lord,
Who daily loads us with benefits,
The God of our salvation!** *Selah*
**Our God is the God of salvation;
And to God the Lord belong
escapes from death.**

(Ps 68:19-20)

We often need an escape from a situation that is declaring death over our purposes and businesses. What we see in the natural may cause us to feel desperate—things are really bad, recessions have hit, there just seems to be no way forward—but great news! Recovery also comes through correcting and adjusting your lifestyle, and the way you live out your relationship with God. Your ordered conduct releases the salvation of God, which happens to include an escape plan with benefits that are downloaded daily into your situations. It is wonderful to know that you have a way out when God is involved. Your lifestyle does play an important role in the open provision that can potentially come to you and accelerate your situation. You may feel that something more dramatic would be necessary to see acceleration in your business and life. Lifestyle may not present that feel for you, but it should never be underestimated.

The way we live definitely opens the door to financial opportunities. For example:

1. Honour

The broader meaning of *to honour* is *to regard something with respect or to keep your obligation on what you have said*. To **honour** the principles of God's Word is to keep them; to place a high value and emphasis on them and to allow them to operate in your life. You demonstrate that by making room for them. Honouring a gift ministry or the set man over you, for example, means you accept what God has sent you to grow spiritually as God's plan for you.

Jesus **"...came to His own country..." (Mark 6:1)** which obviously suggests He was known in that area, and taught in their synagogue on the Sabbath.

> **And many hearing Him were astonished, saying, "Where did this Man get these things? And what wisdom is this which is given to Him, that such mighty works are performed by His hands! Is this not the carpenter, the Son of Mary, and brother of James, Joses, Judas, and Simon? And are not His sisters here with us?" So they were offended at Him.**
>
> **(Mark 6:1-3)**

Familiarity is the cause of many miracles being lost to a situation. That is why it is imperative to develop in your lifestyle the trait of *honour*. When we honour the gift ministry sent to us, we show acceptance and respect for what that person carries from God and this becomes the seed bed for the miraculous. Jesus, the anointed Son of

God, who was being used to perform the most amazing miracles anyone had ever seen, came home, and because the people saw Him as they originally knew Him (just one of them), they became offended at Him.

"Now He could do no mighty work there, except that He laid His hands on a few sick people and healed them. And He marveled because of their unbelief. Then He went about the villages in a circuit, teaching."

(Mark 6:5-6)

People needing to recover in life or business should take serious notice of this. Familiarity was the reason that the power of God was kept from working the way it could.

But Jesus said to them, "A prophet is not without honor except in his own country, among his own relatives, and in his own house."

(Mark 6:4)

In another lesson, Jesus taught that if you receive a prophet in the name of a prophet, you would receive a prophet's reward. **(Matt 10:41)** What a person carries from God can be yours. It can be released with effectiveness into your circumstances. The anointing the priest holds is the ability to bless. **(Num 6:22-27)** What a prophet has to share will work the miraculous in your circumstances. What he says from God will materialize. Place the right honour on the principles or gift ministries God has for you and you will have their reward. Let your life convey this fruit and you then position yourself for of the miracles of God. Never take the anointing of God lightly. It has the power to break yokes and cause new life to emerge. If you want to receive from an anointed gift ministry, then honouring where God has anointed will see the release of the miraculous into your situations.

2. Diligence

Diligence is a careful, persistent, and attentive approach to your work ethic. It is not erratic or inconsistent in application. Going about your work with this understanding brings great reward from God. It is a trait that our lifestyles should contain and reveal a good measure of excess. God respects diligence—and the story of the talents in **Matthew 25** shows this clearly. The servant who was not diligent with the one talent he had been given was rebuked, and what he had was taken from him and given to the one who showed the most diligence. The talents were given, **"...each according to his own ability." (Matt 25:15)** This servant had no excuse for he was well able to produce with what he was given. He clearly was lazy in his approach to its application and had to endure the consequences. Hard work is the essence of success. A lifestyle that is not prepared to work hard and have excellence attached to it is not likely to generate lasting success. **(Proverbs 4:3; 12:24; 13:4; 21:5)**

3. Mercy Giving

Giving out of a heart of mercy also carries much weight with God. When you have sufficiency to give and you share with those who don't have, you demonstrate an understanding of mercy. Those who *have* normally tower above those who *don't* and it is within your power to help and give mercifully to those in need. It is your choice. This form of lifestyle moves God. Remember He is always in ascendency over us and has the power to be merciful to those who can't help themselves. When we practice this trait as part of the way we conduct ourselves, it does open up for us a return of mercy when we need it. **(Ps 37:21-22)**

4. Generosity

Having a generous spirit opens up incredible promises.

> **"So let each one give as he purposes in his heart, not grudgingly or of necessity; for God loves a cheerful giver. "**
>
> **(2 Corinthians 9:7)**

> **"But a generous man devises generous things, And by generosity he shall stand."**
>
> **(Isaiah 32:8)**

You show the fruit of generosity when you work out ways to be generous. Businesses should include in their budgets sums of money that have been devised to help those businesses that are struggling. When you get to this place as a lifestyle practice, God promises that because you have operated in this way you will stand in tough economic times when others around you collapse. So then knowing this principle and knowing that this is your practice will give you a certain amount of confidence when pressure in the marketplace arises. Somehow God will show you how to stand and last through the impending, uncertain markets with their erratic trading. Your lifestyle of generosity will cause you to remain intact.

5. Blessing Your Man of God

Abraham showed that blessing Melchizedek with the tithe from the portion of the spoils of war was a lifestyle practice that bore much fruit. We read in **Hebrews 7:6** that it unlocked the promises of God over his life. There seemed to be a lifestyle practice in earlier times that you never received from a man of God without taking a gift with you. There is definite merit in this practice, but it should not be a coerced one as it is often done today. Abraham demonstrated that raising his hand to God (making the point that God's financial principles would make him rich and no other) was certainly the lifestyle that produced much blessing in his lifetime. **(Gen 14:22-23; 24:1)**

6. Taking a Gift to the Gift Ministry

As with blessing your man of God, taking a gift to the gift ministry seemed to be a lifestyle practice in early biblical times. When the people wanted their own king and Samuel appointed Saul as the first King of Israel, **(1 Sam 10:21-27)** there were some who hated the choice **"...and brought him no presents..." (v27)**. So taking a gift to a gift ministry showed acceptance and respect. If you didn't, it revealed that you despised the choice as a gift and therefore were in danger of missing out on the reward he carried.

There are numerous examples of taking a gift to validate this as a lifestyle practice. When Saul was out looking for his father's donkeys and had not had any success, he decided to approach the prophet of God in the nearby city. The first thought in Saul's mind was, **"But look, if we go, what shall we bring the man? For the bread in our vessels is all gone, and there is no present to bring to the man of God.**

What do we have?" (1 Sam 9:7) He did eventually find something to give, and in return, received the prophet's reward, and more, in Saul's case. Others examples can be found in:

  a. **Genesis 43:11-13**
  b. **2 Kings 5:5**
  c. **2 Kings 8:8-9**
  d. **2 Chronicles 9:24**
  e. **Philippians 4:15-19**

7. Sacrificial Giving

Ruth sacrificed her life in the sense that she put hers on hold whilst she took care of her mother-in-law, who had returned home with nothing to sustain her in this phase of her life. Ruth gave up the right to go back to Moab and possibly meet a new husband after her own personal loss when she decided to follow Naomi back to Israel and sacrificially care for her. She was prepared to become a foreigner in a strange land and risk all the dangers that it proposed. She would become a gleaner in the harvest fields and shared the scraps with Naomi to keep them both alive. Even when she was blessed she made sure she first separated what would be Naomi's portion. **(Ruth 2:18)** This lifestyle of sacrificial giving was not unnoticed and it made a way for both her and Naomi to break out of where they were. Boaz was very complimentary:

  a. He recognized the sacrifices she had made. This reputation preceded her. **(Ruth 2:11; 3:10)**
  b. He prayed a blessing prayer over her that related to a full recovery for her. **(Ruth 2:12)**

c. He arranged unexpected bundles of blessing to lie in her path, so she would not fail to collide with them. **(Ruth 2:16)**

A sacrificial lifestyle will not go unnoticed. God will see it and cause others who can help, to see it as well.

8. Support of Church Mission

Again this is a choice you make freely but it brings God pleasure. You don't have to do anything extra, but Paul made it clear that those who saw the value of partnering with the purpose of the church mission would have all their needs met by God in Christ Jesus. In other words, take care of what is valuable to God, and then what is valuable to you would also be taken care of. **(Phil 4:15-19)**

9. Value the Kingdom of God

Jesus came preaching the kingdom of God. He announced that God's rule was now come to replace what was currently in place. In **Matthew 6:33**, Jesus made it clear that seeking **"…first the kingdom of God…"** was a priority in life. Figuring out how the kingdom of God worked—what keys opened which doors—all led to **"…and all these things shall be added to you…"** The passage is really about showing the value of not needing to chase after the things that we think will make life better for us. Having things does not mean we have arrived. Chasing the rule of God on the earth is the key that adds to you. This is a lifestyle that is worth working towards. It keeps a discipline on the temporal things we think we need whilst it unlocks the secret of having things added by God. When God adds to you, it is without stress or striving. Making the kingdom of God a priority in your life is a healthy lifestyle practice releasing what needs to be **'added'** to it.

10. The Lesson to a Thief

Paul spoke to the church in Ephesus in **Ephesians 4:28**, and he particularly addressed those who used to steal. He taught that people should go out and get a job so that they could support themselves and not have to steal anymore, making sure they had something to give to those in need. Why would Paul encourage giving a portion to those in need? He well knew the meaning of **"Give, and it shall be given to you..." (Luke 6:38)**. When you give to those in need, God always makes sure it comes back to you, usually magnified. Paul taught this principle to those who relied on stealing to make a living. He underlined the value of God's principles and encouraged them to try it, because they work. Success would deliver them completely from the need to steal, when they saw the effect that giving a portion away regularly had on their financial returns.

This can become a lifestyle trait that we utilize as well. Giving a portion of our paycheque away purposefully every month will show long-term dividends of God's returns that we cannot monitor. They will just keep on arriving from various untiring sources.

UTILIZING THE PRINCIPLES TO ACCELERATE LIFE

Lifestyle does contribute significantly to financial returns. The principles may not deal with money exactly, but then they do result in God releasing blessing to you and opening opportunities for you to progress and increase proportionately. Ordering your lifestyle correctly will always result in God showing His salvation in your circumstances.

Acceleration is possible. It just may not be as one-dimensional as you think. It may require that you increase your thinking to more of the out-of-the-box approach, and perhaps even beyond. God has significantly more ways to bring recovery and acceleration to us than what we may want to believe. But RECOVER we can, and WITHOUT FAILING.

ALL THINGS ARE POSSIBLE WITH GOD.